HIDDEN TREASURES

YOUNG WRITERS

SURREY

Edited by Katie Coles

GW00691841

First published in Great Britain in 2002 by
YOUNG WRITERS
Remus House,
Coltsfoot Drive,
Peterborough, PE2 9JX
Telephone (01733) 890066

HB ISBN 0 75433 834 7
SB ISBN 0 75433 835 5

FOREWORD

This year, the Young Writers' Hidden Treasures competition proudly presents a showcase of the best poetic talent from over 72,000 up-and-coming writers nationwide.

Young Writers was established in 1991 and we are still successful, even in today's technologically-led world, in promoting and encouraging the reading and writing of poetry.

The thought, effort, imagination and hard work put into each poem impressed us all, and once again, the task of selecting poems was a difficult one, but nevertheless, an enjoyable experience.

We hope you are as pleased as we are with the final selection and that you and your family continue to be entertained with *Hidden Treasures Surrey* for many years to come.

CONTENTS

Christina Georgallou	89
Miranda Buckland	90
Ashleigh Wood	91
Rosie Sibthorp	91
Claire Edwardes	92
Emily Austen	93
Sabrina Stefan	94
Florence Wade	94

Parkside School

Jeff Brown	95
Roy Lambert	96
Tom Stock	97
Nico Thompson	97
William Lander	98
Max Bowerman	98
George Allen	99
Oliver Bailey	99
Nicky Jillings	100
Alex Fletcher	100
Tom Hancock	101
Kaleem Ali Khan	101
Felix Smith	102
Lloyd Johns	102
Raphael Leon	103
Matthew Clark	103
Robert McManus	104
Daniel Kitcatt	104
Patrick Harman	105
Michael Fregnani	106
Faris Toosy	106
Tristan James-Weed	107
Freddie Campbell	107
James Oakley	108
Adam Bodini	108
Paul Custance	108
Jack Worsley	109
Brian Rud	109

Royal Alexandra & Albert School

Weyfield Primary School

Samantha Warren	185
Sadie Lewis	185
Sam Watts	186
Shannon McWhinnie	186
Jake James	187
Arron Nye	187
Teri-Lianne Brazil-Halls	188
Sian Young	188
Charlotte Bundy	189
Rebecca Gray	189
Kirsty Salmon	190
Samantha Davies	190
Jade Spinks	191
Matt Kelly	191
Tom Howard	192
Emma Ness	192
Jake Sullivan	193
Chantelle Dixon	193
Sarah Bell	194
Niall Campbell	194
Ruth Browton	195
Jasmine Blackburn	195
Chelsey O'Mahoney	196
Paul Fenton	196
Katherine Hope	197
Jamie Varney	198
James Stevens	199
Taren Hewer	200
Jeysie Mallett	200
Sarah Liddicott	201
Bradley Carey	202

Worplesdon Primary School

Liam Jackman	202
Thomas Bates	203
Elliot Mitchell	203
Ben Beagley	204
Caroline Lowe	204

The Poems

A DEMON

A demon entered our city
dressed in blackened robes
she was a shadow that crept after us
she was a lady who brought danger
she was a chant that cursed our death

We weren't aware of her magic
we weren't aware of her magic
we weren't aware of her magic
which could kill our souls

She brought death
death that was dark
she brought death that ripped flesh from our bones
she brought the fear that haunted our lives
forever, forever

She ruled our lives for many years
we were her slaves for mercy
we were forced to build temples
in her honour, in her honour
we had to treat her as a goddess

Our king became a tramp
our queen became a housewife
because of that selfish, sly, sleazy witch

But there was a birth
a birth that brought joy in every way
it was the cherry on every cake
it was our hope when all was dark.

Hannah Moore (10)

A Christmas Recipe
(For having fun at school during the festive season)

Take one special school and a bunch of happy children.
Add a twinkling tree
And a host of heavenly carols.
Toss in a seasonal pantomime
(Oh no we won't! Oh yes we will)
And a bucket of excitement.
Spoon in a dollop of fun and games,
Secrets, cakes and raffles.
Stir well.
Take a mouth-watering turkey lunch,
With an abundance of mince pies and crackers.
Throw in some funky music and glitzy party gear,
A few *ooohs and ahhhs!*
Mix well with cards and festive wishes.
Carefully add one small babe, a proud mum and dad,
Adoring shepherds, worshipping kings
And what have you got?
The spirit of Christmas.

Emily Mills (11)

My Mom

I have the best mom
She is not like other moms eating gum
She loves to do art
And she loves driving a shopping cart
I love her curly hair
And she really takes care
I love her voice
And her choice
She is full of fun
Yes, that's my mom.

Anuj Patel (10)

HIDDEN TREASURE

As pirates sail down the calm blue sea,
They hold in their hand a golden key,
We want to find a chest or trunk
They say
'We're going to find the treasure today
Rubies, sapphires chunks of gold
Down the years these stories have been told,'
But when they got there they saw the trunk,
When they rummaged through they heard clunk, clunk, clunk
But all that was in there was,
Bits of feathers and bits of trees
All this is nature we can find,
Treasure that is yours and mine.

Antonia Lewis (9)
Micklefield School

HIDDEN TREASURE

At the end of the rainbow,
What treasures it holds,
There's diamonds and rubies,
There's silver and gold.

I can't wait to get there,
I'll be as rich as can be,
All the money and jewels,
Will all be for me.

So many colours up there in the sky,
All of those colours up there so high,
Red colours, green colours, yellow and blue,
A beautiful rainbow waiting for you.

Nicola Henderson (8)
Micklefield School

HIDDEN TREASURE

Shovels dig,
Finding fossils.
How much fun you have
Finding fossils.
Dinosaur bones in caves.
In big caves or small.
Finding fossils,
Oh! What fun.
Digging deep,
Down to the ground.
Finding fossils,
Oh! What fun.
Discovering Romans and Egyptians,
Or even dinosaurs.
You might find them in the sea,
Or in caves!
Oh! What fun.
Diving down wells.
Oh! What fun.
Getting tired,
Time to go to bed.
But just can't wait
For another exciting day
With so much fun.

Christopher Mooney (8)
Micklefield School

HIDDEN TREASURE

As I sail on my boat,
I'm feeling quite sea sick,
The waves are bobbing up and down,
I've got to get to shore quick!
Oh! There's an island but where's the town?
I get off suddenly
And slowly lie down,
I feel quite lonely,
But wait! What's at my feet?
Is it a colouring, no it's a map!
Maybe if I follow it there may be something to eat,
Look I'm still wearing my cap,
As I walk my shoes fall off,
Ouch! That hurts,
Oh! No! Now I've got a cough,
Oh look I've found the place,
I dig with my hands,
Dig with my face,
The treasure is wrapped in rubber bands,
Wow! That's a lot of treasure
And look there's a lamp,
I think I'll rub it with pleasure,
Look a genie I hope it won't stamp.

Charlotte Colquhoun (9)
Micklefield School

HIDDEN TREASURE

Whilst I sail in search of the chest,
Dreaming I am the richest in the west,
Hope I find the treasure soon,
Hope I find it before it's noon.
My boat is floating ever so high,
The sky is stormy, I hope I don't die.
Sailing on to a desert isle,
Don't want to get eaten by a crocodile!
Made it to Treasure Island,
Where do I go?
Ah, the map that I hold,
It is very, very cold.
I have found the treasure,
The chest is very old.
I'm opening the lid,
Wow, it's gold!

Alexander Hazelton (8)
Micklefield School

FIRE!

Fire is good and fire is bad,
The best is it's warm the worst is it burns.
When it's good it is very relaxing,
But when it's bad it will be distracting.
It will start to smoke,
Just try not to choke.
The flame will rise,
Don't jump in surprise.
Nine, nine, nine,
Is the fire brigade's rhyme.
Fire is good and fire is bad.

Eleanor Fry (8)
Micklefield School

THE DUMB MONSTER

Under your bed there's a big, fat, hairy monster,
He's dumb and got no brain at all,
He's a chatterbox but cries like a baby,
People describe him as fat, clumsy and greedy.
He smells like he doesn't believe in showers,
His clumsy feet step on everything in my room,
He's purple, blue and definitely not scary,
Even though he's ten times bigger than you.
All you have to do is flick him and he cries like a baby,
He's even a scaredy cat if you can believe it,
At night you go up to him and say *'Boo!'*
He screams and hides behind your door.

Naima Abbas (9)
Micklefield School

AT THE THEME PARK

At the theme park it's great,
You should go sometime.
There's a tidal wave where you get wet,
There's a water slide, *whoosh*, down you go,
There's a roller coaster with screams and shrieks,
There's a ghost train which is spooky.
Candyfloss and lollipops with a hot-dog,
Ice cream and chocolate,
All lovely things.
Nice, delicious sweets,
Freshly home-made,
What's good about it,
Is you get it free.
The theme park's great,
Everyone loves the theme park.

Clarissa Hearn (9)
Micklefield School

PIRATES

Pirates are dangerous and pirates are exciting,
They swing on ropes and slash with a cutlass,
With blazing eyes they steal and they rob.
I think they're frightening, what do you think?

Pirates smell like old cheese.
They never have a bath
They're selfish, they're greedy, they're wicked and evil.
With the captain's parrot flapping against the sea salty air,
Speeding along, fighting the wind, what a boat!
They smile with glee when they're on the sea,
I think they're frightening, what do you think?

Pirates are nasty
They would lock you up if you touched their treasure,
But remember they're thieves.
With their swords, they cut you in half.
I think they're frightening, what do you think?

Sebastian Willacy (8)
Micklefield School

HIDDEN TREASURE

Bubbling potions,
hold the clue,
green, yellow, red and blue,
what treasure do you hold?
The glass ball,
tells the future,
magic sweets make wishes come true.

Potions make a pop,
mix and stir,
make lots of magic things,
polish the glass ball,
until it shines,
to do all this,
you have to be
a sorcerer!

Katharina Clark (9)
Micklefield School

MY BROTHER

My brother is brown haired with hazel eyes
He's messy and muddy, cheeky but cool
He likes orange but I like purple
He gels his hair every morning
He is annoying but funny
I love my brother.

My brother loves ice hockey
He always goes to matches
My brother is quite smart
He's very good at RE
He loves art and DT
He's the best brother in the world.

My brother annoys me by not letting me hold his hamster
He spies on me
He annoys me when I'm doing my homework
Most of all he watches what he wants on TV
But I love my brother.

Sophie Hall (8)
Micklefield School

HIDDEN TREASURE

A pirates' chest of gold,
Is not the only treasure.
The fog and the mist,
Is what I think is treasure.
It is see-through and solid,
Everything is hidden.

A pirates' chest of gold,
Is not the only treasure.
Rainforests and jungles,
Is what I think is treasure.
They're green and they're wet,
Everything is hidden.

A pirates' chest of gold,
Is not the only treasure.
Under the sea,
Is what I think is treasure.
The swirls and the rocks spread your imagination,
Everything is hidden.

A pirates' chest of gold,
Is not the only treasure.
You're unique,
Is what I think is treasure.
Your feelings and thoughts,
Everything is hidden.

A pirates' chest of gold,
Is not the only treasure.
But our glistening eyes,
See what we think is treasure.

Stephanie Wright (9)
Micklefield School

HIDDEN TREASURE

Ships jumping on the waves,
The coral reef is down below.
With fish and sharks,
At last! The pirates land.
'X' marks the spot,
Follow the map.
Dig, dig, dig,
Clang! The chest!
The chest, let's open it,
Let's open it,
Diamonds, Rubies
Brooches, jewellery
Coins and Silver!
Gold!

Harriet Gibson (8)
Micklefield School

HIDDEN TREASURE

The pirate smiled with glee,
As he saw the sea,
Scrub the deck!
When it needs a peck.
You walk through a cave
And grab a spade,
You open the top,
It gives a pop.
You take one pace,
With a smile on your face,
Nothing there,
How, when, where?

Jonathan Willacy (8)
Micklefield School

HIDDEN TREASURE

The pirate, the pirate
He's cold and he's wet
It's dark and it's gloomy
Now how about that.

It's really quite rocky
And also so wet
But one-legged Jim's not frightened - not yet!

It's wavy, it's rough
And then what a shock
We hear a great crash,
The boat's hit a rock.

All of us rushing,
Rushing about
Trying to swim
To try and get out.

I swim and I swim
It's grey and it's dim
I look for an island
But can't see a thing.

At last I feel sand beneath my feet
I leave the cold water, oh! What a treat
Up on the sand a huge chest I find,
Brimming with trinkets and treasure of all kinds.

Georgina Mitchell (9)
Micklefield School

HIDDEN TREASURE

Pirates going out to sea,
Early in the morning,
Want to be first there,
So dig for treasure and see what's there,
Gold, money, what nice things,
Dig, dig to make you rich,
Black patches over your eye,
To make you look more scary,
Want to frighten people away,
So you get it all to yourself,
Get the necklace and everything nice,
Want to get rich,
It would be such fun,
Follow the map, it gets you there,
Even though you have to travel over sea,
You'll get crowns, gold bracelets,
Ancient jewellery, all things you want,
You just can't wait,
But you can't get the riches,
Because you haven't found the key,
Looking for it everywhere,
Round trees, round rocks,
Where is it? Where, where, where, where?
You've found the key!
Now follow the map again,
Reached the treasure,
Now to dig, dig, dig, dig, dig,
Here's the treasure,
Open the box,
Just a *cake.*

Katie Stephens (9)
Micklefield School

FIRE!

The fire is blazing,
It is glowing and sparkling,
Then the fire starts to crackle,
It is very warm and cosy,
It's getting quite noisy.

I see some fireworks,
They are very colourful,
They are exploding,
It is bonfire night,
People are lighting Guy Fawkes,
It is getting really loud.

The fire is destroying everything,
The buildings are falling down.

Charles Steedman (9)
Micklefield School

MY SISTER

My sister's sometimes annoying,
She's sometimes fun,
She likes playing with dolls
And pretending she's the mum.
She's sometimes shy
And sometimes fun.

My sister's only eight,
Her favourite thing is to paint,
Her favourite colours are yellow
And purple too.
She's full of fun
And happiness.

My sister's not that great,
There are some things about her that I hate,
When she makes a loud noise
And I'm doing work.
She's sometimes horrible
And sometimes nice.

Abigail Boar (9)
Micklefield School

MY BIRTHDAY

It's my birthday!
I'm nine.
My sister got me a necklace,
My mummy got me a bracelet.

On Sunday it's my party,
I'm really excited.
I'm having some friends over
To stay the night.
Sophie's the main one,
I'm going to have the best birthday ever.

I feel really happy, tingly and fresh.
I couldn't get to sleep,
Even with a grown up,
Even with my daddy.

Hannah Taylor (9)
Micklefield School

HIDDEN TREASURE

T   is for *treasure* which is all around us, we just need to look.
R   is for *rainbow* with colours like gems.
E   is for *elephant* which I long to see.
A   is for *apples* shining red on the tree.
S   is for *Sybil* my special little dog.
U   is for *unicorn* a magical creature.
R   is for *rare* which all treasure is.
E   is for *Earth* the most precious planet in the universe.

Megan Clarke (9)
Micklefield School

THINGS I WANT - BUT I WANT IT NOW

I want a bicycle, rollerblades. Oh, I nearly forgot, designer clothes.
    But I want it now.

I want my own mansion, oh and a telly or two.
I want my own bath with foams.
    But I want it now.

I want a trip to Disneyland in Florida,
my own private suite and limousine.
    But I want it now.

I want my own computer and I want to be up on a stage to be seen.
    But I want it now.

I do not want a Game Boy or a PlayStation 2
but how do I get this to you?
I want a family, friends and their love.
    But I *have* it now.

Jenny Goodwin (9)
Notre Dame Prep School

THE DRAGON'S LAIR

D angerous, enormous beast, who could eat us all as his feast,
>Dirty and scary, but he is very hairy.

R ound and round the maypole, the dragon is actually very playful.
>Raging fire, he looks so fierce, but he really doesn't like
>getting his ears pierced.

A ero chocolate, mmm, yum, yum, but the other dragons like
>meat and gum.
>All the animals they kill are carried to their lair,
>but this special dragon just couldn't care.

G olden hair like Goldilocks, but oh what a chatterbox.
>Gently tickles his little pets, but sometimes loses his bets.

O liver is his name, acting is his game. Ollie is always kind,
>but sometimes he loses his mind.

N aughty but nice, his favourite food is rice.
>Nelson his brother, who else, is there another?

Kimberley Wood (8)
Notre Dame Prep School

THE SONG OF THE NIGHTINGALE

Last night I swear I saw a feathered little kite,
swiftly float through the trees.
Then, suddenly landing on a mossy branch,
it sang the most beautiful song.
So sweet, so dazzling, with the moon's light,
shining on its colourful feathers.
I don't think anyone had ever heard such a song,
so soft, so light, since that night.
As the song of the nightingale sings to this day,
I wonder if anyone will see such a sight as I saw.
The song of the nightingale faded into the dark of the night.

Suzanne Murray (9)
Notre Dame Prep School

How To Choose A Hair Band

How to choose a hair band,
I really do not know,
I have to go to school now,
So I can't be slow.

I don't want a ponytail,
I don't want a bow,
I don't want some hair slides,
But it's nearly time to go.

I can't wear a sparkly one,
It's not allowed at school,
I can't wear my fluffy one,
It makes me look a fool.

How to choose a hair band,
I haven't got a clue,
Red, yellow, pink, no,
It will have to be blue

Blue is my favourite colour,
I like it lots and lots,
I have a dozen plain blue bands
And one of them has spots.

I have to choose a hair band,
It's nearly time to go,
I will just close my eyes and pick one,
It's the fluffy one, *oh no!*

Philippa Dawes (9)
Notre Dame Prep School

MY TREASURES

Off I go to Dreamland,
It's time for me to go,
No time to stay or play around,
I really shouldn't say no.

Off I go to Dreamland,
I'm really nearly there,
No time to waste and daydream,
I really should be there.

Off I go to Dreamland,
Time is running out,
We've got to get there soon enough,
Or the world will die out!

Off I go to Dreamland,
Pack up ten things,
What should I take with me,
Memories, love or rings?

Off I go to Dreamland,
Where shall I go?
No time to run or stare about,
The rivers near will flow.

Now I'm here in Dreamland,
There's patterns on the floor,
My family's my hidden treasure,
Oh how I adore!

Natasha Allwork (9)
Notre Dame Prep School

MY PLAYFUL PUPPY

Melting, big, brown eyes
A golden, silky coat.
My soft, cuddly puppy
Is my true delight.

Chasing balls she twists and turns
She plays until she flops.
My golden ball of energy
Is my dream come true.

She chews on shoes and old socks too,
She bounces round the room.
My mum says she's a pickle
But I still give her a tickle.

I had a disco for my birthday
My dog was the best DJ.
She played *Who Let The Dogs Out*
And didn't run away.

Jenny O'Neill (8)
Notre Dame Prep School

CHRISTMAS TIME

Snowflakes falling from the sky,
Little robins flying high,
Crunchy snow upon the ground,
Children singing all around,
Tinsel is hung around the tree,
Church bells ring merrily,
Santa comes in a sleigh,
Everyone enjoy your special day!

Hannah Stainton (8)
Notre Dame Prep School

ANOTHER DAY OF SCHOOL

Opening the gate
Playing in the playground
There goes the bell
Pulling out my chair
Hearing the desk slam
Now the teacher's yelling
Packing up for maths
Everybody say your seven times tables
Packing up for English
What is a verb?
Time to go home
Leaving the playground
Opening the gate again.
Bang.

Katie Walsh (8)
Notre Dame Prep School

THE FLOWER

One bright flower hidden,
In my bedroom.
Growing brightly,
With beautiful colours on it.
The pine took my breath away.
So slowly it grew
And how honoured I was
To see such beautiful flowers.
The colours were pink, lilac and green.
The pearls inside glittered so brightly
I love it!

Anastasia Hodge (8)
Notre Dame Prep School

MY FRIEND MAX

My friend Max is a cat,
He scratches on the mat.
He loves fish
In his dish.
My friend Max is fat.

Max has a friend called Snowflake
Who likes to eat toffee cake.
He's fat like Max,
He plays with wax
While Grandma tries to bake.

Max, Snowflake and I
All like chocolate pie.
Chocolate is best
While we rest.
We'll be friends until we die.

Siân Johns (7)
Notre Dame Prep School

CHRISTMAS TIME

Snowflakes falling on the trees
making them icing white
Outside carol singers stand and freeze
singing on a winter's night
Inside people hang their sack
presents overflowing till it's full
Santa's coming, Rudolf's back
isn't Christmas cool!

Rochelle Williams (9)
Notre Dame Prep School

BEDROOMS

My room is tidy and neat.
In your room, you can't even see your feet
And your room is a mess!
There's no place you can dress.

My room is true blue.
Your room is white as flour
And your room is red as a flower.

My room is as big as a tree
And your room is as tiny as me!

But all these rooms are special, as you can see.

Madeleine Van Vleet (8)
Notre Dame Prep School

THE ROBIN'S TUNE

I was sitting in the garden
When I heard this sweet tune,
The robin was sitting on the tree
In the middle of June.

He sang so sweet
And he looked so neat;
I could lie there all day,
Just watching him play.

Soon the sun will set
And I'll have to go home,
I will leave my poor robin
Alone on his own.

Sabrina Burgess (8)
Notre Dame Prep School

DISNEYLAND

Minnie Mouse
Mickey Mouse
Pluto
Pooh.

Goofy
Donald Duck
Tigger too.

Sleeping Beauty snoring
Eeyore Eeyore-ing
Snow White sleeping
And Buzz is beeping.

Dumbo flying
Dale and Chip lying
Alice choosing
Mad Hatter losing.

The Beauty is lovely
And the Beast is ugly
Piglet singing
And Peter Pan winning.

Disneyland is a fun place to be!

Rachel Hogge (8)
Notre Dame Prep School

HIDDEN TREASURES

In my heart I have a box of hidden treasures,
Inside it lie memories of holidays,
And good times with friends.

My hidden treasures are deep inside of me,
They are smiling faces,
And sunny beaches.

My hidden treasures help me when I'm sad,
They help me through the day and night,
They get me through tough times.

My hidden treasures are locked up in a box,
And when I open it
I get filled with happiness.

Sophie Omissi (11)
Notre Dame Prep School

FACES

Some are round
Some are square
Some are oval
But never bare

Some are black
Some are white
Some are yellow
But always bright

Some are smooth
Some are rough
Some are hairy
But sometimes tough

Some eyes are blue
Some eyes are green
Some eyes are brown
But can always be seen

Some ears are big
Some ears are small
Some ears are hairy
But never cool.

Madison Hornsby-King (8)
Notre Dame Prep School

POOR OLD GRAN!

I have a gran, who is very unlucky,
She falls into mud, that makes her mucky.
She tried to buy charms
But every time, she got hit by arms.

She is blown by wind every day of the year,
Everywhere she goes, the sky is not clear.
Whenever she talks she always gets hit,
By people around, so she calls them a twit.

When she is at the zoo the lions want to eat her
And every time she notices this she says things like *'Ooer!'*

She thought she would never be lucky, but one day,
Guess what she found, a four-leaf clover,
Which at last made her lucky and proud.

Sara Ji Yen Koay (9)
Notre Dame Prep School

THE FLOWERS

The flowers are nice, they are all so pretty
They're nice and small, yellow and blue
And all the colours you could think of.
They dance, dance and dance till they are quite worn out
Then they close their eyes, say goodnight, close their petals
And fall asleep through the night.
When it is morning they start to sing
Wash their teeth and faces and start to have fun again.
Some play, some do not but they are always happy.
When rain comes they cheer and go to sleep.

Victoria Saez-Benito (8)
Notre Dame Prep School

A RECIPE FOR A PERFECT FRIEND

First get a huge bowl,
Spoon in some playfulness,
Next mix in some happiness,
Add a few secrets,
Tip in a bowlful of kindness,
Stir it together with a pinch of cheekiness,
Shake in some cuddles here and there,
Then fold in some comfort,
Blend in some helpfulness,
Bake in the oven for thirty minutes
And to finish, squirt on some giggles
And there you have a perfect friend.

Megan Ranger (8)
Notre Dame Prep School

HIDDEN TREASURES

In my heart

I keep all my treasures,
My family's happy faces,
My mum, my dad, their love,
I don't know what I would do
Without my best friend Georgina,
She is my life, my friend, my family,
I also have a dream at night,
To swim with the dolphins.
My teddy must be the one who I really adore the most
The one who I can talk to,
But all I want in the world is peace,
Happiness and kindness.

Louise Stroud (11)
Notre Dame Prep School

BATHING

Go to the changing room to change my clothes
Squeeze into my pink swimsuit and ready to go
Jump into the pool and watch the waves
As my sister and I race across t'other side.

Run to the steps leading to the slide
Pushing and shoving to get there first
Zooming down with an almighty splash
Down into the water then bobbing up.

Race to the stairs to start again
Run to the Jacuzzi instead this time
(Changed my mind as I often do)
Jumped into the bubbles - oh! So hot.

Sprint to the changing room
To change back again
Dash back to the car
And drive back home.

Lana Miller (8)
Notre Dame Prep School

JUDO

Judo is fun, Judo is great,
Judo makes you go *'Hoy ya!'*
But if you get far too close,
You might be ending up saying *'Aaahhh!'*

The idea of Judo is,
To get to the highest grade,
But if you do not succeed,
The teacher will give you a grenade!

Sometimes Judo is funny,
Sometimes it's serious,
But very often you get squashed,
So it's very hilarious!

Judo is fun, Judo is great,
Judo makes you go *'Hi ya!'*
But if you get squashed,
You might end up saying *'Ha, ha, ha!'*

Nicole Nelson (9)
Notre Dame Prep School

UNDER THE SEA

Under the sea there are
Seashells, seashells,
Sounds like ringing bells, ringing bells, ringing bells.
Ooh look at that coral reef, coral reef,
My shell, your shell, his shell, her shell,
Oh you little thief, thief, thief!

Under the sea there is
A great white shark
Down in the depths
Where it's dark, dark, dark!

Under the sea
The jellyfish are gliding.
On top of the rocks
There are limpets slip, sliding.

Under the sea
Eels lurk in caves.
Their fishy prey rising,
With the rhythm of the waves.

Alice Turner (8)
Notre Dame Prep School

BABY, BABY

Baby
Baby, baby,
Baby, baby, what
Baby, baby, what do they do?

Baby
Baby's bottles all around,
Whilst we are creeping,
Trying not to make a sound.

Baby
Baby, baby will you burp now?
There that's good,
That wasn't so hard, tummy is better.

Baby
Baby, baby let's go to bed
And lay down your little, sweet head,
With bear and bottle and blanket too.

Baby
Do they smile and gurgle all day long,
Whilst I sing a lullaby song?
Baby you're getting tired, close your eyes
And I'll kiss you *goodnight.*

Grace Lewis (8)
Notre Dame Prep School

A DOLPHIN

Dolphins dive in the sea,
Swimming fast, swimming free,
You can see them from afar
Shining like a shooting star!

Their bodies glimmer in the sun,
They're happy, playful and having fun.
They disappear out of view,
They're loveable and friendly too!

Sophie Weber-Hall (7)
Notre Dame Prep School

DINOSAURS

'Run for your lives!
The dinosaurs are coming!'

Purple ones, green ones,
Yellow ones and blue.
Quickly hide in the loo,
They are coming after you!

'Run for your lives!
The dinosaurs are coming!'

Spotty ones, stripy ones,
Scaly ones too.
Keep your voices very quiet,
Don't give them a clue.

'Run for your lives!
The dinosaurs are coming!'

Angry ones, fierce ones,
Snarling and roaring loud.
They're out to squash you,
So scare them out of view.

'Run for your lives!
The dinosaurs are coming!'

Anthea Crown (8)
Notre Dame Prep School

I REALLY WANT AN ANIMAL

I really want an animal,
Black, brown or white,
I really want an animal,
To sleep in my room at night.

I badly want an animal,
Cute, lively and fun,
I badly want an animal,
To take to the park for a run.

I desperately want an animal,
Brave, strong and quick,
I desperately want an animal,
That can do a backward flip.

I urgently want an animal,
That can hop, skip or fly,
I urgently want an animal,
That can jump to the sky.

I finally got an animal
And decided to call it Roo,
I finally got an animal,
You've guessed it . . .
A lovely kangaroo!

Amelia Walker (9)
Notre Dame Prep School

SILLY STORIES

In the playground
On my own,
Reading my joke book alone,
Then I find silly stories,
A little round thing lying on the ground.

It's a squashed slug,
I would have put it in a mug . . .
Well, that's my story,
I won't say more.
It's not too nice . . .
I will keep it a secret, will you?

Emily Stubbs (7)
Notre Dame Prep School

TEDDY BEARS

When the teddy bears came to my house
They were chattering and nattering and squeaking like a mouse!

They spilled their eggs on the kitchen floor
And they did more mess and more.

My mother got all angry
And shouted at them really loudly!

She told them to pack up and leave,
She screamed, 'Please, please, please!'

But the teddy bears did not listen,
They stayed up watching television!

'Why don't we go to the beach,
And bring back lots of special treats?'

We played a game in the sea,
And the teddies found a key.

So I said, 'Why don't I push you out in the sea
So you can find a door that will open with the key?'

The teddies thought this was a lark,
But then got swallowed by a shark!

Jennifer Rose (9)
Notre Dame Prep School

HIDDEN TREASURES

I am high in the sky
Floating on the clouds
When suddenly I bump
Into something hard
It's a wooden box all tattered and torn
I open the box and sparks fly out
They are visions of my special secrets,
The ones I really treasure.
My family is waving at me
I don't know what to say.
Then all my dreams come zooming out,
The ones I love so much.
My pets are there, the ones that died
And I start to cry tears of joy.
This is my box, the one I love
With all my treasures in it.
I run back home to show my mum
The box that I have found
But the box has disappeared
So I say to myself, 'Well never mind,
Those treasures are still in my heart.'

Grace Macleod (10)
Notre Dame Prep School

MY PONY

I have a pony, he is soft and grey,
He nuzzles me and plays with me all day.
He gallops on the grass as I walk past,
In a show he never comes last.

Georgia Davies (7)
Notre Dame Prep School

MY MESSY DOG

My messy dog rolls in the mud.
He doesn't care where.
He goes into people's gardens
And annoys all the cats.
He wakes me in the morning,
He doesn't care one bit.
He hogs the fire.
My neighbours always come to complain
When he barks in the morning at sunrise.
He mucks about in the mud
And sometimes I join him.
My mom calls me to take a bath,
Whenever I play with him.
He's a lovely dog deep down inside him.
I always have to wash him in the morning and at night,
For he will always be my favourite dog.
I care a lot.
If he dies I'll bury him in the back yard,
So he'll always be by my side
And that's my messy dog.

Ellie Brown (8)
Notre Dame Prep School

MY PUPPY MAISY

It would be so cool
If I came home from school
And found a puppy in the hall.
It would be the best thing ever for me.
I would call her Maisy and when I walked her
She would eat up all the daisies.

Catherine Hallala (7)
Notre Dame Prep School

SPRING IS HERE

This morning when I awoke,
The blackbird at the window spoke.
'Wake up lazy bones, spring is here
I've been singing loudly in your ear.'

I ran to the window and looked outside,
Winter had gone and the sun shone in the sky.
Little crocuses were peeping through,
'Mum!' I called, 'Look at the view.'

I got dressed and went to the farm,
Newborn lambs in the cosy barn.
Butterflies fluttering all around,
Bunnies hopping on the ground.

The fresh smell of new cut grass,
Easter is approaching fast.
Chocolate eggs are a wonderful treat,
The next season is summer, I can't wait for the . . . *heat!*

Annabelle-Rose Steen (9)
Notre Dame Prep School

HIDDEN TREASURES

My hidden treasures are kept inside me,
I think about them day and night,
I never let them past me,
I lock them up inside my head,
I think about them when I'm in bed.

In my heart are my treasures,
I will never forget them until I'm in heaven.

Victoria Kershaw (11)
Notre Dame Prep School

HIDDEN TREASURES

I was walking along when I saw a box,
I wondered for a moment what it was,
It could have been a treasure chest.
I took it back home
I put it with treasures of my own.
I put in the chest
The smiles of my family's face,
The feeling of swimming with a dolphin,
Fun I've had with my best friend Louise.
I put in the chest,
The laughter on my summer holidays,
The fun that I've had building snowmen.
I put in the chest
Generosity for my friends.
I put in the chest,
Kindness for my family.
I put in the chest,
Peace.

Georgina Hodge (11)
Notre Dame Prep School

SNOWDROPS

S   nowdrops, snowdrops cold, cold white,
N   ever here on a warm summer's night.
O   h snowdrops,
W   here are you in the summer,
D   ried up in your drooping stem?
R   eally why aren't you with all the
O   ther summer flowers? Think of them all
P   ink and red.
S   nowdrops it's summer now, you should stay in *bed!*

Sophie McKinney (9)
Notre Dame Prep School

DREAMS

When I go to bed,
I rest my head
On a lovely fluffy pillow
And snuggle under
A cosy blanket.

When I shut my eyes,
My imagination runs wild
And I dream of
Monsters and vampires
And everything you can think of!

Sometimes I dream
Of lovely things
Like fantasy places,
That I've never seen.
With flowers and vines
Which go on and on
And fairies and elves
And beautiful queens.

Then all of a sudden,
I open my eyes.
I'm back in my bedroom,
For a new day.
I've finished my dream
Until tonight,
When I'm back in my bed
And turn off the light.

Daniella Jones (9)
Notre Dame Prep School

My Mystical Creature

It's got a head like an elephant -
A tail like a mouse.
Feet like a donkey -
And a neck like a giraffe.

It hisses like a snake -
And hoots like an owl.
It crows like a cock -
And moos like a cow.

So even if she's weird,
Or has a long beard -
She's my favourite creature,
Come along and meet her.

Lana de Beer (9)
Notre Dame Prep School

The Robber

The robber is very fast,
He whooshes right past.
He is so smelly
And wobbles like a jelly.
He wears all black,
As he carries a sack.
He's stolen jewellery and so much more,
But his two left feet put him on the floor.
Out comes Daddy
And shouts, 'Help! Paddy!'

Priya Patel (8)
Notre Dame Prep School

MY TREASURE

My treasure is my tree house
I wish you could see it.
It's built around a tree
So there is plenty to see.

My treasure is my tree house
It has a balcony to sit on
And a staircase to climb
Although that does not rhyme.

My treasure is my tree house
You can sleep in there.
You're near the outside
But could be anywhere.

My treasure is my tree house
Friends come up to tea
There is lots to do up there
And an awful lot to see!

Lucy Mitchison (8)
Notre Dame Prep School

HIDDEN TREASURE

In my one and only box
Are the things you'll never see
Chocolate boats and wooden docks
That will never be.

I'll sail away to Hawaii
Never to be found
Only my wooden box and me
Sailing round and round.

Dancing in the moonlight
All by myself
I'll wait there all night
Hoping to meet an elf.

Everything seemed to be
So real but now I see
That nothing's ever like that
Unless it's in a dream.

Emma Horsnell (11)
Notre Dame Prep School

MONKEY

I have a monkey
His name is Ben
He sits with me
In my home-made den.

We laugh and play
Every day
I hold him tight
All through the night.

He's my best friend
And when I'm low
He's always there
To say hello.

So that is all
About my friend
Which now brings
Me to the end.

Emily Rymer (8)
Notre Dame Prep School

THE HUMAN LIFE

I woke up one day in my nice, cosy bed,
Stretching my arms as high as I could,
Opening my curtains wide,
My eyes were squinting,
Because of the dazzling sunshine,
I ran downstairs as fast as I could,
To collect my breakfast,
Whoosh in the corn flakes,
Splash in the milk.

Eat it up quick,
Run back upstairs,
Sling my pyjamas off,
Sling my uniform on,
Pack my school bag not forgetting my PE kit,
Rush in car wait till you hear about the seat belt,
Smash in the seat belt, oh no, it broke,
Clamber into the back,
Click the seat belt in.

And then we're off,
Mum takes the lead,
Then another car in red takes over,
Zoom down the school lane,
Screech at the car park turning,
We're at school now,
Do a few lessons and go and find Mum,
Come home, slip my school uniform off,
Put my PJs on
And slip into bed.

Chloe Caddie (9)
Notre Dame Prep School

THE FAIRY

She flutters round me up and down
And I see she wears a little crown.
I wander up and down the street
Staring in the sky at a fairy I wish to meet.

There she is swaying in the sky,
I think how I wish to fly
Showing her round, faithful wings,
And then gently she sings.

I am the Queen of Fairyland,
I wear a crown of gold.
I go around visiting friends
And have flower petals for my bed.

At night I see a star in the sky,
And that is when the fairies fly.
They have a little fairy parade,
And they all have fairy lemonade.

The Fairy Queen flies by,
And flutters up into the sky.
I reach out my hand to touch her
But too late, she's gone.

On the way to school
I look up to the sky,
There is a little fairy
Fluttering by.

Amy Macleod (9)
Notre Dame Prep School

MY CAT HAS A HAT

My cat has a hat
To hide his head that is so fat.
He wears it when he goes to sleep,
He wears it when he's going to weep.
He holds it in his furry paws,
The dog next-door tries to steal it with his claws.
He has it when he eats his dinner
Although he knows it won't make him much thinner.

I think we'd better leave our cat
For really he does love his hat,
And his head is quite fat.

Daniella Richardson (9)
Notre Dame Prep School

HIDDEN TREASURES

Under my pillow
I keep my nana's old scarf she wore in the war
I dream that my grandpa comes back for me
My baby sister saying, 'Hello Issy.'

Under my pillow
I keep Jenny's porcelain dolls
Jenny's Hazel, her favourite toy,
Jenny's mini Goldie and Beanies too.

Under my pillow I keep
My dream.

Isabel Goodwin (10)
Notre Dame Prep School

MY SPECIAL FRIEND

I have a very special friend, his name is Doggy Doo,
I really, really love him and I think he loves me too.
I cuddle him when I'm feeling sad and when Dad's had a fit
And also when my sister's given me a great, big walloping hit!

I take him everywhere I go,
To lots and lots of places.
Seeing people everywhere
With happy, smiling faces.

I don't know what breed of dog he is,
Or if he's girl or boy,
But what I really, truly know is
He's my cuddly toy!

Louise Edwardes (8)
Notre Dame Prep School

FUNGI

I'm deadly
and I'm poisonous,
I'm fiery-red and bad!
I suppose you've heard of my
cousin, he's such a good thing,
but I
am not
that, I
am very,
very, very
bad!

Eleanor Hall (7)
Notre Dame Prep School

HIDDEN TREASURES

Buried deeply in the sand,
There is a box with hidden treasure,
With millions of diamonds and jewels,
Just waiting there for someone to find.

I read a map and find the place
And I dig and dig and dig,
I find the box and open it up
And find . . .

Two gold coins, three red jewels,
Four diamond rings and five glittery dresses.

I take the box with all the treasures
And walk home as happy as ever
And make it back for the sunset
And for a little cup of tea.

Annabelle Cook (10)
Notre Dame Prep School

HIDDEN TREASURE

On my cloud I will put
The song of a liar bird,
The wave of a panda.

On my cloud I will put
The dance of a leaping dolphin,
The bubble net of a whale.

On my cloud I will put
The bark of a dog,
The tooth of a shark.

On my cloud I will put
The sting of a ray,
A cheep of a chick.

So on my cloud
There will be everything
That means something to me!

Lucy Buck (10)
Notre Dame Prep School

HIDDEN TREASURES

Some hidden treasures to me
Are the sloshing sounds of the sea,
The calming songs from the birds,
The 'baas' from the farmers' herds,
The nice warm rays from the sun,
The warm taste from a fresh bun,
The warm autumn colours, orange and red,
The bouncy feeling from a new bed,
The whispering from all the trees,
The buzzing sound from honeybees,
The sweet smell of a pretty flower,
The high mighty look of a castle's tower,
These are all hidden treasures to me.

Geneva Stanton (11)
Notre Dame Prep School

HIDDEN TREASURES

In a dark, dark world
There is a dark, dark island,
In the dark, dark island
There is a dark, dark cave,
In the dark, dark cave
There is a dark, dark chest,
And in the dark, dark chest
There is a dark, dark box,
In the dark, dark box
There are two pretty bows,
Three golden dresses,
Four glass shoes,
And five gold rings,
And will anybody find them all?

Chezelle Bajwa (10)
Notre Dame Prep School

HIDDEN TREASURES

In my one and only heart,
I keep love for ever
That will never part.

Golden wishes that will come true,
Making it wonderful for me and you.
In my wish, peace for life,
Through the world and ever more.

In my one and only heart
I keep dreams of marshmallow clouds.
And little fairies and golden angels flying over us,
With love in their hearts and joy in their souls.

Jennifer Lewis (10)
Notre Dame Prep School

HIDDEN TREASURES

Hidden treasures under my bed
Or spinning around in my head.
The rocky mountains,
The Spanish sun and rain.

The whole of space,
Nothing in the dustbin waste.
The sun, the moon and stars,
Every planet including Mars.

A holiday in Greece,
A jigsaw with no missing piece.
A million pounds,
A roller coaster with ups and downs.

Vikki Ingham (11)
Notre Dame Prep School

BALLET PRACTICE

I go to ballet every week
To learn a dance for Mrs Leak,
She says 'Bar practice first please,
Bend and stretch to the beat.

Centre work please next,
Now show me your sautés,
And Ellie dear, don't bend your legs
And please do Mo stand up straight.'

Now the music starts to play
And we start to dance away,
Sometimes our teachers like to say
How jolly good we are today.

So home we go to tell our mums
How we danced with our chums.
Can I go to the ballet, Mum,
To see how it is done?

Alicia Cox (8)
Notre Dame Prep School

ANGUS

Adorable face, loving you,
Licking you all over.
Swishing tail, wet nose, little legs.
He barks when I come home.
Looking around, following me, asking to play.
Very cute with soft ears.
Who is it?

My dog, Angus.

Olivia Moss (7)
Notre Dame Prep School

THE CUDDLY KITTEN

Last night there was a kitten sitting on my wall,
The poor kitten was about to have a great big fall.
The kitten did not fall by running to our doorstep,
The kitten wanted to meet somebody.
I ran down the stairs and saw the kitten on the mat,
I said, 'Come on in,' to the kitten and gave it a pat.
I went back to bed with the kitten and said,
'Now what should I call you?'
'Tabby's the name,' said the cat.
What, a talking cat, how cool is that?
I gave it a bed and said,
'Go to bed now.'
'OK,' and then it said, 'Miaow.'
In the middle of the night the kitten started dancing
And the girl started laughing.
'Go to bed,' the girl's mother said.
'OK,' said the girl.

Sophie Bond (7)
Notre Dame Prep School

HIDDEN TREASURES

My hidden treasures are inside me,
I think of them so easily,
They glisten in my head, locked up there,
I stop and think I really care.
Like a snowflake they float by
In the black, velvety sky.
Half of my treasures are my heart,
Love and kindness, is a big part.
Sometimes my treasures I lend,
To my friends that is the end.

Sarah Keeble (11)
Notre Dame Prep School

HIDDEN TREASURE

Sail, sail round the world,
Many times you can see,
Until we find an island right
To hide our treasure.

Round and round,
Past Plymouth sound.
We sailed for many a day
Until we land upon the sand
Of Treasure Island Bay.

'This will do,' the captain said,
'To hide our caskets three.
We'll leave them here for many a year,
And return in 2003!'

Emma Ococks (8)
Notre Dame Prep School

THE MOON

The moon is bright,
The moon shines at night.
If you don't see it, it might come out tonight,
The stars glitter too.
If you wake up in the night
You might see a shine of light
Through your window, through your door.
The moon is high in the sky,
The moon is full of light,
It's a lovely sight,
The moon shines all over the world.

Natalie Voak (7)
Notre Dame Prep School

HIDDEN TREASURES

In my heart I treasure
Hope, for the world to be peaceful,
The environment to stay green,
Love for my family
That will stay in me for ever more.

In my heart I treasure
Special memories from the past,
Of my family's smiling faces.
Respect for the people I know are in Heaven,
Looking down from the white, silky clouds.

In my heart I treasure
Lovely compliments that people say to me,
Promises and secrets that I am responsible for.
Me and my treasures will never part
Because they are all hidden in my heart.

My heart is the most special thing to me,
Most importantly
My heart is filled with my hidden treasures.

Danielle Klijnsmit (11)
Notre Dame Prep School

GOOD OLD SCHOOL

Monday, ballet, girls bar, bras.
Tuesday, cross-country, I've gone so far.
Wednesday, gym, I'm on the rope.
Thursday, religion, good old Mr Pope.
Friday is the best of all,
Do you know why? *It's sports for all!*

Wonderful weekend over, Monday starts again,
Time to share with friends.
Tuesday lunch was awful, couldn't eat a thing.
Wednesday lined up in silence.
Thursday the fire bell rings.
Friday the teacher faints, we all pack our things.

Olivia O'Shaughnessy Tredwell (9)
Notre Dame Prep School

THE THREE FRIENDS

There was a young lady from Bath,
Who always slept on the hearth.
If she went to the zoo she would say to you,
'I would love to see a giraffe.'
And when she had seen the giraffe she would have a bath.

Her friend, she came from Spain,
And loved to dance in the rain.
She gave the umbrella
To a handsome young fella,
And jumped in puddles again!

Her friend was from Peru,
She was dreaming she was eating a shoe,
But she got a fright
When she woke up at night,
And found it was perfectly true!

These friends are incredibly weird
And jump around like deer.
The girl from Peru
Has finished her shoe,
And is eating the King of Spain's ear!

Holly Mahon (9)
Notre Dame Prep School

A WINTER POEM

I wish it could snow every day,
We'd make snowballs and go and play.
We'd grab our sledges and find a hill,
Jump on board, *wow!* What a thrill.

In all my races I come last,
But now I'm racing really fast.
Zooming down the snowy hill
Gives me such a freezing chill!

Some snow is falling on my head,
It's making my face very red.
Now I'm coming to the finish line,
And had such a brilliant time!

And as I pass the finish line
I realise I've won the cup that shines.
I've really done it, I've come first,
I'm *so* happy, I think I'm going to burst!

Charlotte Keefe (9)
Notre Dame Prep School

AUTUMN

In the cold chilly wind,
Silently I was watching
Crispy brown leaves slowly falling.
And while I was walking on the hard grey ground
I was so happy at what I thought I'd found.
There in the mildew of the grass,
Shone a shiny, glowing piece of brass.
It was a hard, round red penny,
In which the future will bring me many.

Ambika Prasad (10)
Notre Dame Prep School

THE FLUFFY KITTEN

The fluffy kitten lies asleep,
I go to have a little peep,
Then suddenly she jumps up quick
And walks to her water to have a sip.

Steadily she walks to her bed
And dreams about the garden shed.
Then up she jumps, she smells her tea,
She turns around to look at me.

She gives me a wink and a big smile
And eats her tea for a little while.
She walks off into another room
And starts to play with a red balloon.

She pounces at the balloon,
It pops with a *bang!*
She runs under the chair,
She's had a scare.

I go over to the chair and call her out,
I pick her up but I cannot shout.
She was only playing and having some fun,
It's no good to feel sad and glum.

We lie on the sofa and curl up asleep,
And Mother comes to have a peep.
She thought she would join us in our dreams,
But instead she wakes us up, we're not very pleased!

Gabbi Brown (9)
Notre Dame Prep School

MY DOG FIG

I have a little doggy and her name is Fig,
She's not too small and she's not too big.
She likes to cock her head on one side, then the other,
And always likes to play fight with my older brother.
She is a black Labrador and she's just over one,
I think she's very cuddly and lots of fun.
She follows lots of instructions from 'down' to 'up' and 'sit,'
And will always do 'roll-over' if she gets a big titbit.
She likes to roll in fox poo, it smells so very nice!
For when she rolls in it once, she'll always roll in it twice.
Our dog is very clever and also very good,
She'll come when we call her, even in the wood.
So now you know my Labrador and I think you will agree,
She's the best dog in the whole wide world and she belongs to *me!*

Emily Godby (9)
Notre Dame Prep School

SPRINGTIME

S   leepy bunnies hop around in the grass,
P   retty flowers smile as woodland animals pass,
R   obins fly away to hide as it is too hot,
I   nside their sett badgers play a lot,
N   ow is the time of the year that we start to go out,
G   etting fresh air we all scream and shout,
T   he Easter Bunny is coming soon,
I   eat my cream eggs with a tea spoon,
M   others take their children on picnics,
E   ndless fun and frolics.

Julia Collins (9)
Notre Dame Prep School

THE BEST PLACE IN THE WORLD

The best place in the world,
I think is Marwell Zoo.
We go there to see the monkeys
Scratch and say, 'Oo oo.'

We go to see the elephants
Make a trumpeting sound.
We go to see the zebras
Sitting on the ground.

We go to see the lions
Making booming roars.
We go to see the flamingos
Scribbling boring laws.

We wanted to see some dark blue whales,
But I don't quite think there are
Any whales round here, if you ask me
They are probably far too large!

We always go to the café
When we are at the zoo,
And we always order pizzas
With chocolate ice creams too.

I like going on the swing boats
And the helter-skelter too.
They whiz you really, really fast
So you don't know what to do!

It is really sad
When we have to go home from the zoo,
But I always know that when we go back
We'll have chocolate ice creams too.

Gemma Dracup (9)
Notre Dame Prep School

THE ALPHABET OF FOOD

A   is apples so rosy and red,
B   is bananas that babies are fed.
C   is the carrots you have for your lunch,
D   is digestives that you like to munch.

E   is for eggs that you crack for your tea,
F   is the fruits that are eaten with glee.
G   is the gravy you pour on your meat,
H   is for houmous, you eat if you're Greek.

I   ce cream is what you eat if you're hot,
J   elly will wobble if you shake it a lot.
K   is the kippers you catch from the sea,
L   is for lettuce that's calorie free.

M   is for mints, you eat after a meal,
N   is for nuggets that make children squeal.
O   is for an orange, round like a ball,
P   is for pasta that's long, thin and tall.

Q   is for quail, a very small bird,
R   is rice pud, on top lemon curd.
S   is for salmon, that smells out the house,
T   is for titbits, you give to a mouse.

U   is une pomme, you have if you're French,
V   is for veg that you grow in a trench.
W   is watermelon, juicy and sweet,
X   is 'xcitement while waiting to eat.

Y   is for yoghurt, strawberry tastes best,
Z   is for snoring, for I'm having a rest.

My tummy is full, I can't eat any more,
I've just been sick, all over the floor!

Tayla Pilgrim (9)
Notre Dame Prep School

THERE'S NO OTHER CREATURE LIKE A DOLPHIN

A dolphin is quite a lively thing,
It jumps about in the sea.
A dolphin is a friendly thing,
I hope it will be friends with me.

It likes a lot of people,
They're not at all like sharks.
Sharks try to kill humans,
In a shark's tummy it's very dark.

I'd like to swim with a dolphin,
I think you would like to swim with one too,
They would let you ride on their back,
I wonder if they're at the zoo.

I so want a dolphin as a pet,
But I do know that you can't.
If I could have one as a pet,
For its food I'd give it a sea plant.

People say they've got a dolphin,
But I know that it's not true.
Do you think that they've got a dolphin?
I'd be very surprised if they do.

Dolphins can jump quite high,
You can see them from a boat,
It looks like they're flying through the sky,
I love their silky coat.

There's no other creature like a dolphin.

Kate Rogan (8)
Notre Dame Prep School

ON MY WAY TO SCHOOL

'Come on,' says Mum, 'it's time to go.'
Oh deary me, I am so slow!
So much to do, so much to pack,
I must remember my blue gym sack.
In the car, we leave at eight,
And pick up Katy near our front gate.
Then into traffic all busy and with noise,
Oh my gosh Mum caught me taking in a toy.
Finally we get off to school,
Never late - well that's the rule.
And on the stroke of nine
All the children stand in a line.
Then into the classroom our teacher rushes,
Very quickly the classroom hushes.
The lessons now start, silent as a lamb,
Another happy day at Notre Dame.

Jade Southwell (8)
Notre Dame Prep School

A BUTTERFLY

A lly the butterfly flew up into the sky,

B ut then she started to cry.
U nder the tree is where she sat,
T ears were shared with a lonely cat.
T hey were so sad,
E veryone else was glad.
R osie was the cat's name,
F or she had lost all her wonderful fame.
L ying in the sun,
Y ou and everyone else was having so much fun.

Alex Yue (9)
Notre Dame Prep School

MY PUPPY

Hello,
My name is Spot.
I am a puppy,
I eat a lot.
I belong to a little boy,
He is so kind, he gave me a toy.
I love him and
He loves me.

I play with him every day,
When my owner comes home
He takes me to the park to play.
He says to me,
'Come on dog,
Come and sit on a log.'

When it is dark
I give a bark.
He takes me home
And says, 'Goodnight Spot,
I love you a lot.'

Julia Wood (7)
Notre Dame Prep School

CAN I? YES I CAN

Sometimes I wonder could I do this?
My answer is, possibly not,
But I do know I must give it a jolly good try.

Because, if I don't I will have not
Given it my very best shot.

Harriet Wilks (8)
Notre Dame Prep School

How I Got My Dog

My mum said one day,
'It's time to choose a dog.'
So she took me to the pet shop
And gave me a gigantic choice,
Big, small, large and tall,
Even one I thought was a mop.

I looked into a puppy pen
Where several puppies lay,
It looked as if they needed to play.
'Oh no!' I groaned as they got up,
They looked like right old muck.
As I looked down I saw the one for me,
A small brown and white puppy.

As we drove home I stroked the puppy on the head.
The puppy I wanted,
It can sleep on my bed,
So that is how I got my dog.

Isabella Rohrbach (9)
Notre Dame Prep School

Autumn Poem

A ll the other seasons have come and gone, now I shall need and
U mbrella indeed.
T he leaves fall from tall trees,
U nlikely you will see the bees.
M ud and puddles along the road to school,
N ever too late for the children to play in this mud pool.

Nikita Patel (8)
Notre Dame Prep School

THE NOTRE DAME RAP

It's the Notre Dame Rap, it's the Notre Dame Rap,
Notre Dame is where I go to study
So that Mummy doesn't have to worry.
We have a school dog called Bonny,
She is very funny.
I enjoy art, ICT and football
Which is in sports for all.
Our head teacher is Mr Plummer
Who is always kind to the kids and their mothers.
So come on everybody clap your hands
And make a sound,
Do the Notre Dame Rap, do the Notre Dame Rap.

Priya Mistry (8)
Notre Dame Prep School

DOLPHINS

Dolphins are smooth,
They're pretty too.
They can be grey,
They can be blue.
They live in the water,
They live in the sea,
They're very friendly to me.

Dolphins are cute,
They're related to whales.
The boats above go hoot, hoot,
You hear about dolphins in animal tales.

Chloe House (8)
Notre Dame Prep School

MY NEW PETS

If I have a goldfish
I'll call her Goldie.
I'll feed her plankton,
And she'll live in a fishbowl.

If I have a gerbil
I'll call her Coco.
I'll feed her nuts
And she'll live in a cage.

If I have a cat
I'll call her Pebbles.
I'll feed her fish (Goldie),
And she'll sleep in a basket.

If I have a dog
I'll call him Bingo.
I'll feed him pigs' ears,
And he'll sleep in a kennel.

If I have a horse
I'll call her Misty.
I'll feed her hay,
And she'll sleep in a stable.

If I have a dinosaur
I'll call him Elliott.
I'll feed him all my other pets,
And he'll sleep in the garage!

Imogen Simmonds (7)
Notre Dame Prep School

A DAY AT SCHOOL FOR ME!

First it's maths,
The worst of all!
It seems all day,
But it's not at all!

Next is English,
The second worst!
I wait until it's over,
Not listening to a word!

The teacher's bell rings,
She says, 'Hands up.'
'Heather, Heather,
It's time to wake up!'

Geography comes next,
My head fell down,
I simply
Fell asleep!

I woke up hours later,
And looked in front of me,
I saw an empty test paper,
'I missed a test paper,' I screamed!

Science comes, my best subject,
A bell rings in my ear,
'Is science over?' I ask.
'Of course it is my dear!'

This is a simple
Day at school for me!
It happens every day,
I hope you don't do this,
Especially if you miss a test some day!

Heather Steinbrecher (10)
Notre Dame Prep School

HIDDEN TREASURES

Some hidden treasures are quite large,
And some are very small.
Some hidden treasures
Cannot be seen at all.

Some hidden treasures are brightly wrapped,
Some are tied with a bow,
And then the hidden treasures
Are ready to go.

Some hidden treasures
Are for pirates at sea,
And some hidden treasures
Are just for me.

My best hidden treasures
That I've ever had
Are my newborn sisters
Who make me so glad.

Kate Bukovec (8)
Notre Dame Prep School

THE LITTLE CHICK

Once there was a little chick
That was the first to hatch,
But when the other eggs came out
They did not seem to match.

One day the mother went away
And left the chicks alone,
But when she came back from the hay
The chicks had all left home.

Now all the chicks are mother hens,
They all have eggs themselves,
They keep them safe in their pens,
And tucked up on the shelves.

Katherine Mundy (7)
Notre Dame Prep School

MY GREAT-NAN

I love my great-nan,
She is very kind.
She is ninety-years-old,
But I think she'll go over one hundred.

She lives in a flat
On the bottom floor,
So her legs don't wear out
Climbing any stairs.

Great-nan loves to dance
And listen to the records.
She loves to have a bath
With lots and lots of bubbles.

She likes fish and chips
And buys great meat
For my sandwiches and breakfast,
I love that to eat.

But best of all
Are the lovely hugs,
And her nice smile
On her soft face.

I love my great-nan!

Millie Jones (7)
Notre Dame Prep School

DREAMLAND

I'm going off to Dreamland
To have a day of fun,
There's lots and lots of ride to choose,
A day out in the sun!

I'm going to the beach today
To climb over the rocks,
Crabs are swimming in the pools,
Oh no I've got wet socks.

The afternoon we spent at the coast
Was the best we ever had,
Boys and girls were playing games
But some of them were really bad.

My day at the coast is at an end,
And I am really sad.
I hope we come again next year,
Then I'll really be glad.

Chloë Rymer (10)
Notre Dame Prep School

GRANDAD

One day I went to Grandad's
And Nana opened the door.
In the lounge I saw him
Lazing in the chair.
'Grumpy Grandad, please wake up.'

Saucy Suzie, what do you want?'
'Grandad, please play a game of chess with me.'
'I will, get the board out.'
'Can I be white?
Grumpy Grandad please play.'

Grandad is old and grey,
But smiled and laughed at me.
'Get the biscuits and make the tea,
But please don't take all day.'

Suzie Forbes (7)
Notre Dame Prep School

ANIMALS - ALL ABOUT RABBITS

Rabbits like eating carrots, cauliflower and celery.
Wild rabbits live underground.
You must give rabbits fresh water every day.
Rabbits like hiding and then being found.
Rabbits are very soft.
Rabbits are very fluffy.
When you give them a bath they get all puffy.
When rabbits are in danger
They put their ears down and stop.
When they know it is safe
They run around and hop.
Rabbits like running.
They sleep on hay,
When they wake up
They come out and play.
When my rabbit is hungry
He likes oats and wheat.
When he is really good
I have him lots of treats.
My rabbit lives outside
In a big hutch,
I let him run every day
And he likes it very much.

Jasmin Berg (7)
Notre Dame Prep School

BOOKS

I was looking for a hidden treasure
But I wasn't sure where to go,
So I stood on platform nine and three quarters,
And ran into Nicholas Flamel.
After Hogwarts and a bad case of stripes
I went on to learn how to live for ever.
I've met a great white shark, a blue ringed octopus,
A cobra and porcupines.
I've been all around the world,
Then I discovered that the treasure is with me all the time.
The treasure is the books I read,
They are hidden in my mind.

Sarah Poletti (8)
Notre Dame Prep School

THE FUN BOOK

The fun book has a horse, pig, goat and hare,
I think we should really share.
I think it's good if we read a book,
And put my coat on to the hook.
I can thread some string
And sew a dress,
But reading is the thing I like best!
You imagine what it can be like . . .
And just pretend you're there alright!
You can run, shout, push and hit,
But I like reading more than a bit.
I like drawing and colouring too,
But the greatest thing to me
Is to read, read, read.

Charlotte Tully (8)
Notre Dame Prep School

MY PUPPY

The animal I am talking about
Is cuddly and fluffy,
And is still a puppy.

I take him for walks around the park,
Then he is very happy and barks.

He is not very fast when he runs,
And makes roly-polies and jumps.

His legs are short and his body is long,
It is a sausage dog, nothing is wrong.

Looking at me with his brown eyes,
Glistening in the night
Sometimes they give me a fright.

But then I realise, it is Benny
My puppy, which I love with all my heart.

Celina McElevey (8)
Notre Dame Prep School

MY RABBIT ROSIE

My rabbit Rosie
Is rather nosy.

She hops round your feet
Hoping for a treat.

If nothing is found
She looks all around
For something yummy to eat.

Tilly Charnleybeal (8)
Notre Dame Prep School

DOLLY THE HORSE

Dolly the horse is tall and brown,
She is beautiful and good.
Her eyes are bluey-green
And has nice, tappy feet.

I hear a crunchy sound
And some food fell out.
She is really scared of cars,
They make her back up.

She likes to trot a lot.
She likes to jump a lot.
She likes to canter a lot.

She has beautiful feet.
She has a very beautiful tail,
And she is my favourite horse.

Hannah Lie (7)
Notre Dame Prep School

I SEE IN THE SEA . . .

I see in the sea
a turtle skimming the sea.

I see in the sea dolphins spinning,
twirling, whirling, rolling and jumping.

I see in the sea waves in rolling grace
as blowing sand hits my face,
but now feet pass
meadows of green grass.

Harriet Hall (7)
Notre Dame Prep School

HIDDEN TREASURES

Off I go to Dreamland,
I really cannot wait,
I hope I find some hidden treasure,
Oh that would be great.

Off I go to Dreamland,
Some gold and silver I can sense,
I will soon be rich now,
Oh that would be great.

Time to leave Dreamland,
It's been a lovely day,
I haven't' found any treasure yet,
I might find some on the way.

I wake up in my own bed,
The next morning I find
There is no treasure under my bed,
It must be in my mind.

Layla Allos (9)
Notre Dame Prep School

MY PONY

My pony is called Spot,
He is black and white and dotty.
He loves playing in the fields
And having good meals.
He loves eating hay all through the day,
He is my best friend, right to the end.

Nicola Wood (7)
Notre Dame Prep School

NOTRE DAME SCHOOL

I go to Notre Dame School,
It is very, very cool.
Mr Plummer's the headmaster,
There is a school nurse if you want a plaster.
The school dog, Bonnie, is so sweet,
Mrs Pollard says my work is neat.
I eat my lunch in the school hall,
And I go swimming in the school pool.
At breaktime I play bat and ball,
Don't play rough is the school rule.
Best of all I like ICT and art,
In my uniform I look smart.
The ponies down the lane are so cute,
If only I had my riding boots.

Chelsea Rand (7)
Notre Dame Prep School

MY MUMMY

My mummy is very kind
And she does lots of things for me,
She lets me stay up late at the weekend.

My mummy takes me to parties
And helps me when I am stuck on my homework.

My mummy tucks me up in bed
And reads me a story.

My mummy is the best mummy
In all the world!

Clare Macmillan (7)
Notre Dame Prep School

ON THE BEACH

On a shining beach,
Filled with golden sand,
The sun shining down
Across my bare hands.

On a shining beach,
Water splashing by,
Lots of different creatures,
Even larger flies.

On a shining beach,
People playing ball,
How can I reject it,
Although I am not that tall?

On a shining beach,
Night is never light,
Families eating dinners
Under the shining night.

Jan Ying Lee (9)
Notre Dame Prep School

RAIN, RAIN

Rain, rain it's nice to see
How you fall so beautifully,
And fill the lakes with water.
You make the plants grow
And give us lots of water.
Now I want to play outside
And look at what you've done.
Bad rain, bad rain
I don't want to see you again.

Sonia Smith (7)
Notre Dame Prep School

HIDDEN TREASURES

There is a town,
In that town there is a place, in that place
There is a street, in that street there is a road,
Down the road is a house, in that house
There is a room, in that room there is a bed,
Under the bed there is a chest, in that chest there is a box,
On that box there are some locks,
Finally I opened it but nothing was inside.

I looked on my bed which was in my room,
The room in the house, house by the road,
Road in the street, street in the place,
Place in the town . . .

But wait, I see something in my mind,
It is my imagination I needed to find.

Belinda Doyle (11)
Notre Dame Prep School

GEORGIE MY PUSSY CAT

I love my little pussy cat,
She's soft and warm and sweet.
She licks herself down
To keep her fur nice and neat.
She sits on my lap and purrs away,
But sometimes she just likes to play.
She loves to keep warm on my bed,
And when I go to sleep she curls up by my head.
Georgie is my pussy cat,
I love her more than words can say,
I cuddle up to her and feed her every single day.

Philippa Stevens (8)
Notre Dame Prep School

WHAT'S INSIDE?

What's inside? Who knows,
Let's find out.
A star which has landed on a mountain
With snowflakes trickling down,
A music box which looks like a little girl
Was a ballerina who was just waiting to dance.
A little brown box,
What's inside?

What's inside?
A lock of hair,
A best friend's necklace,
Your family's voice,
One drop of the rainforests rain,
One touch of good dreams,
It's just a box.
What's inside?

Nikki Brouwer (9)
Notre Dame Prep School

THE PLAGUE STRIKES!

Rats are creeping into bags of flour,
People are dying hour by hour.
Black spots mean they've caught the plague,
A white cross on the door means *stay away!*
Soldiers stop people leaving town,
The plague must not be spread around.
Doctors try to help the ill,
They do not have a magic pill.
The priest sees those who are dying,
Throughout the town dead bodies are lying.

Lois Sharland (7)
Notre Dame Prep School

HIDDEN TREASURE

Off I go to wonderful Dreamland,
I hope it's going to be great.
I wonder if there's any treasure,
I hope I'm not too late.

Off I go to Dreamland,
I'm walking down a silvery path.
Oh what is that shiny chest?
I hope it's the one I want.

I have reached the end of the path,
'Oh look, oh look,' I say, 'there's a silver treasure chest
But someone is blocking the way.'

I crouch down to see who it is,
And it is Mr Beetle.
'Excuse me Mr Beetle, may you go away?'
And he replies, 'Oh yes I will,'
And so he goes off to play.

And now I have opened the treasure chest,
Inside is diamonds and emeralds.
'Oh how wonderful,' I say,
'I wish I could do this every day,
But it would not be the same.'

Tania Kumar (9)
Notre Dame Prep School

MY PET

I have a little budgie
His name is simply Blue.
His feathers are so smooth and sleek,
I love to see him eat his millet
As though he has never been fed,
He enjoys it very much.

I give him grated carrot and apple,
He fluffs up his feathers,
And preens himself all day.
He loves it when it's time to sleep,
We cover his cage for a rest.
He likes to look in his mirror all day,
And likes to jump around.

Rebecca Copson (8)
Notre Dame Prep School

MUM MAKES ME TIDY UP

Mum makes me tidy up,
I really don't know why.
After hours of tidying
I heave a great big sigh.

Mum makes me tidy up,
I really don't know why.
After days of tidying,
I feel ready to die!

Mum makes me tidy up,
I really don't know why.
After weeks of tidying,
I want an apple pie.

Mum makes me tidy up,
I really don't know why.
After years of tidying,
I'm allowed to stop!

Milly Maudsley (9)
Notre Dame Prep School

I HAVE A TREASURE BOX

I have a treasure box
Sitting in my room,
I put my toy car in it,
It goes, *zoom, zoom!*

I have a treasure box,
It's really very cool,
I put special things in it,
Like my big red ball.

I have a treasure box.
My brother thinks it's sad,
I tell him it's just cos he hasn't got one,
He says he's so glad.

I have a treasure box,
It cheers me up when I am down,
I put lovely things in it,
Even my circus clown!

I have a treasure box,
Now the night has come.
I think I'll go to bed now,
And dream of treasured fun.

Alexandra Aljoe (10)
Notre Dame Prep School

SEALS

A seal's fur is white and grey,
Their eyes are very dark.
I love to watch them in the sea
And hear their funny bark.

A seal loves to swim and play
In the icy sea.
I wish that I could have one day
A little seal with me.

Dorothy Robertson (8)
Notre Dame Prep School

AUTUMN LEAVES

Autumn leaves are blowing,
All the rivers are flowing,
Bluebirds are singing
In their leaf-made nests.
Sweet, fragrant flowers are blooming
In the autumn sun,
Where the breezy wind blows.

Fresh is the water falling
Through clouds from heaven,
Crisp leaves are brittle
Underneath pleasant squirrels' paws.
Butterflies flitter,
An acorn is opened by the squirrel's sharp claws.

The sun disappears behind the dark clouds
And stars poke their heads out of the dark sky.
Soon, it's gone quiet, everything is still,
The world's gone to sleep,
Even the wind is softening down.
Autumn leaves stop blowing,
Soon a cold breeze comes and . . .
Autumn has gone forever,
Winter is here.

Sarah Irvine (10)
Notre Dame Prep School

HIDDEN TREASURES

My hidden treasure is always near me.
As soon as I wake up, the first thing I see
Is my hidden treasure having a cup of tea.

It's happy, it's sad, it's jolly, it's fun,
It takes me everywhere when I am glum.
When I am hungry, it fills my tum.

When it parts with me I am sad,
But when I see it again, it makes me glad,
I try so hard not to be bad.

At night I sit and think of her
While my cat sits and purrs,
But my hidden treasure doesn't have fur.

My hidden treasure is very precious to me,
But sometimes I forget to tell her you see.
Guess who? My mum is the treasure that holds the key.

Gina Trinchese-O'Reilly (10)
Notre Dame Prep School

MY SCHOOL

Notre Dame is my school,
Everyone is nice not cruel.
Every day I learn and play,
Having fun day by day.
I love the school,
So do you,
Because we are best friends too.

Holly King (8)
Notre Dame Prep School

HIDDEN TREASURE

Hidden treasure, where can it be,
Under the toy box or under the sea?
I need a map for me to look,
Finding my treasure is like reading a book.
Oh, where could it be,
Under the toy box or under the sea?
I've started my quest,
It's a great test.
Could it be there or could it be here,
Or is it not very near?
My hidden treasure, here it will be,
And it's not just only for me.
Over the rainbow, under the toy box and under the sea,
Where could it be?
There it is right in front of me.
Yes it's the world!
For us all to see.

Natalie Elgar (11)
Notre Dame Prep School

STARLIGHT

S   tarlight shines very brightly against the night sky.
T   u-whit tu-whoo go the owls.
A   round her all is black.
R   iding across the sky is Santa Claus.
L   ight sprays across Santa's white beard.
I   nside the star, happiness hopped around.
G   ardens could be seen below.
H   appy feelings went whizzing about the dark sky.
T   hanks and praise to God.

Sophie Dracup (7)
Notre Dame Prep School

HIDDEN TREASURES

During the day
It is out to play,
At night,
It is not bright.
Sometimes it rains
And it is not there.
Some people do not care
If it is or is not there.
I do, I care, I wish it
Would always be there.
Now the people stand and stare
And they all start to care
If it is or is not there.
My hidden treasure is the golden sun,
It brings light and joy to everyone.

Tasmin Crabtree (11)
Notre Dame Prep School

HIDDEN TREASURES

It's gold, it's beautiful,
It's shaped as a heart,
A chain around my neck,
Will never let us part.

I keep it in a box
That is under my pillow,
It makes me feel warm
Instead of very chilly.

It shines so bright
In the starry night,
So I can find
My way without a light.

It's gold, it's beautiful,
It's close to my heart,
Yes, it's a locket,
Like I said we shall never part.

Ruth Sherrington (10)
Notre Dame Prep School

A TALL MOUNTAIN

A tall mountain,
With a sprinkle of love,
Tall in the sky, high above.

A hazelnut box,
What is inside?
A smile of love,
Or a ring for me?

A hazelnut box,
What is inside?
A rainbow across the sky
For friendship,
Love
And peace.

Maedbh Lyons (10)
Notre Dame Prep School

ADVENTURES

I'm going to go on an adventure,
It's going to be big and great,
No explorers are going to be better than me,
Not even explorers I hate.

I will tackle trolls and monsters,
As I get better I might start
Killing Martians and killing fleas,
That would be so smart.

I shall go on wobbly bridges
And save the classic princess,
All alone in the dark and wet,
I would be a mess!

Suzanne Templer (10)
Notre Dame Prep School

WHAT IS INSIDE?

A light brown box,
A wooden box,
A snow-covered mountain,
What is inside?

A best friend's necklace,
A picture of my family,
A smile from my family,
Pretty jewellery,
A sparkling star from the dark sky.

Gracie Han (9)
Notre Dame Prep School

My Special Treasure

A golden box,
That looks like a star,
With green velvet inside,
Waiting to be opened.

What is inside?

A picture from my family,
And a bit of hair
From my family.

What is in my imagination?

My family would be there,
Waiting for me
To be with them.

Jacqueline Schoenfelder (9)
Notre Dame Prep School

What Is Inside?

A light brown box,
A wooden box,
A snow-covered mountain,
What is inside?

Photograph of my best friend,
Picture of my family,
Picture of my toy,
A blue flower,
My family.

Kei Suganuma (9)
Notre Dame Prep School

THE PRINCESS BOX

The princess box
So small nothing can fit in,
But I've seen her putting her jewellery on,
And I've seen the box.
It looks so pretty,
But what can be in it?
What can be in it?

It could be an engagement ring
Waiting for her long-lost love,
Just waiting there,
Just waiting.

It could be her baby,
It could be her baby's first curl.
What could it be?
What could it be?

Eleanor Daly (9)
Notre Dame Prep School

HIDDEN TREASURES

My hidden treasures are small and white,
Perhaps they swim alone by night?
By day, they shelter snug and warm,
Safe against the sudden storm.

Softly creeping down I go,
Down to where the waters flow.
Peeping through the waving reeds,
I watch them follow, their mother leads.

Splashing water, feathers glimmer,
Gliding through the light, they shimmer.
Dipping heads, paddling feet,
Hungry calls, they search to eat.

Kneeling still I look around,
One stray fluff ball aground.
Hidden treasure, close to me,
I know that I must leave him free.

Ricarda Steele (11)
Notre Dame Prep School

HIDDEN TREASURES

Over the mountains far, far away,
Treasure lay hidden away.
In a hot, sandy desert,
Or even in a dark wet wood,
I looked and looked as far as I could.

Is it shiny, is it bold,
Is it even something gold?
I won't stop looking,
I will never give up,
Because I want it just too, too much.

I'll need a map to lead the way,
I'll need a charm to make me stay,
But most of all I will need my brain
To find my treasure that I will keep
For ever and ever again.

Christina Georgallou (11)
Notre Dame Prep School

OFF I GO TO NEWLAND

Off I go to the Newland,
Oh, I don't know what to take.
I want to take everything,
But I only can take ten.

There are so many things,
I could take toys,
But I need to take some feelings,
I need to take everything,
If the world is going to end!

I am going to take some friends,
I need them to play with.
I have to take food and water,
Or I don't know what I'll do!

I have to take my family,
I really want my pets,
I want to take my talent,
It's music, I think it's great!

I want to take my best toy,
He is called Harry.
I need memories to remember
The world and the past.

I have to have feelings,
I need them to love.
I think I'm done now,
Oh no, I've got two more to go!

I really have to take love
And I almost forgot,
Oh dear, I can't put that down.
I'm done!

Miranda Buckland (9)
Notre Dame Prep School

HIDDEN TREASURES!

My hidden treasure lives close to me,
It stays with me, always with glee.
It's very precious, can't you see?
My hidden treasure makes me, me!

It shines so bright, like a glowing star,
They were to me and still they are,
The glowing star in my heart
Will never die and never part!

They make sure they are always there,
Even when I don't seem to care.
Who I am talking about I see each day,
They make me feel a different way!

Ashleigh Wood (11)
Notre Dame Prep School

NIGHT

As I look out of the window,
The moon is shining brightly,
Clouds scudding across the sky,
Yet the wind is whirling swiftly.

As I look out of the window,
The grass is blowing briskly,
Trees swaying to and fro,
Yet the wind is whirling swiftly.

As I look out of the window,
The leaves are revolving round,
Yet the dawn is coming,
But the wind is still whirling swiftly.

Rosie Sibthorp (10)
Notre Dame Prep School

OFF I GO TO DREAMLAND

Off I go to dreamland,
It's nearly time to go!
I hope it will be really fun,
And don't forget the gum!

Oh no! look at Big Ben,
It's nearly striking ten!
I have to catch the train at midnight,
Or else I could be late.

Oh help me Mum,
I need to pack,
We need to get out of this old shack!
Oh no! the clock has just struck ten!

I need to pack this fat old hen,
I need to hurry up now.
Time is running out,
I'm really trying not to shout,
But this is getting silly.

I think I'll have to leave behind
Anything that's frilly.

The time is ten,
But I started at seven.
Oh well!
I'll have to catch the bus
To get there by eleven!

Claire Edwardes (10)
Notre Dame Prep School

THE BOX

I'm going to start a hobby,
I'm going to have a box,
I'm going to put ten things in it,
I'm going to make it lock.

I'm not putting sweets in it,
I'm not putting my clothes in it,
I might get some old toys
And I'll put my favourite baseball in.

I might put my favourite shoes in,
Their heels are very high,
And I'll put in my fluffy slippers
That I got from my granny and grandad.

I'm putting in my shiny book
That I've written all my secrets in,
I'll put something in every night,
Then it will be full.

When my box is full to burst,
It will take my old things out
And put them in the bin,
And then I'll start filling again.

And when I get home from school,
I'll play with something from the box,
I'll play with something new each time
And neatly put it away.

Emily Austen (10)
Notre Dame Prep School

HIDDEN TREASURES

Up the road a great sight to see,
It's big, it's grey, it's on four legs.
It can see in the dark, it can see in the light
And to me it shines so bright.

On his back he's got two things
But you know they are really wings.
He says to me I am a star,
But I don't believe him because he is bigger than you are.

You can get him big and small,
But I like him because he's tall.
I say to him I love him so,
Oh please, oh please, oh please don't go.

If you listen just a bit more,
A flying horse through the sky will soar.

Sabrina Stefan (11)
Notre Dame Prep School

OFF I GO TO DREAMLAND

Off I go to dreamland,
I hope it's going to be fun,
I'm only allowed to take ten things,
I think it will be great.

Off I go to dreamland,
Gold, silver and bronze.
The clouds are dusty at night,
They're going to be really shiny.

Off I go to dreamland,
I really cannot wait.
Tick-tock, tick-tock goes the grandfather clock,
Oh great, I'm here.

Off I go to dreamland,
I've only just got here,
Everything is going great.
Oh no! I have to go now.

Florence Wade (10)
Notre Dame Prep School

LIGHTNING FLASHES

Lightning flashes,
Thunder clashes,
Silver blades pounce down from the clouds,
Cracking and roaring with a deafening sound.
The wind howls,
Rain falls down,
I fight and push against the gale,
As rain pelts my face, making it cold and pale.
Rivers flood,
Dirt turns to mud,
Banks burst as water races down,
Sand bags piled outside in towering mounds.
As the lightning flashes,
Thunder clashes,
Wind howls,
Rain falls down,
Rivers flood
And the dirt turns to mud.

Jeff Brown (11)
Parkside School

SCHOOL

School, school is such a bore!
When I come in the morning,
It is always very boring.
Assembly is very long,
For we have to sing a song,
And if you don't sing along,
You'll be miserable through the day.

School, school is such a bore!
On the way to the lessons,
My bag is like a stack of hay
And teachers give us piles of work,
If we don't do what we're told.

School, school is such a bore!
In PE,
Although the academic lessons are at rest,
The physicals will come next.
You run for metres,
Swim for yards,
And then you will have something to smile for!

Four o'clock is coming near,
We will go to the classroom
And shouts will fill your ears,
Until the teacher comes
And your classmates hear.

School is not a bore now
For it is time to go home.
We will not groan,
We will go home!

Roy Lambert (10)
Parkside School

School

School, school,
What a horrible place!
I'd love to hide my face.
All the teachers tell me off
Just because I'm not a *boff!*
(If you feel sorry for me,
please send me 50p!)

School, school,
What a horrible place,
Always running in a very big race!
Running round the games field,
Running round the school,
At the end of a very long day,
I'd love to jump in a pool!

Tom Stock (10)
Parkside School

School!

School, school, such a horrible place,
You're not allowed to hare around the place!
The teachers are so strict,
I feel like I'm getting pricked!

School, school, on a rainy day,
I don't feel like going anyway!
At playtime on a rainy day, the puddles
Are very deep. Can't even see my feet!

Nico Thompson (10)
Parkside School

THE SCARECROWS

T he solitary people on sticks are
H orrible, hideous images flapping in the wind,
E erie zombies in their ragged clothes.

S cary hawks circle the sky,
C arefree scavengers waiting for the kill.
A sinister wind blows across the field,
R aising scarecrows from the dead.
E arthly carnivores risen fresh from the dark,
C orrosive killers ready to strike.
R olling thunder cracks across the heavens,
O verhead, the lightning flashes,
W hipping fear in and around,
S inister killers scanning the ground.

William Lander (9)
Parkside School

SCHOOL!

Here I'm sitting in an English lesson
On a Friday afternoon,
Waiting, like a man at a bus stop,
For the bell!
Then I suddenly started to snooze . . .

When I woke up
And looked around,
No one was there!
Not even a pencil.

Max Bowerman (10)
Parkside School

AUTUMN TIME

Autumn time has come,
Roads full of leaves
Crackling when you tread,
In autumn time.

Playing with the leaves,
Jumping in the sun,
Rolling on the grass,
Because it's autumn time.

No time to stay inside,
All the time to play outside,
Leaves in the pool,
It's autumn time.

Leaves on the roof,
Leaves on the ground,
Running through them all around,
Because it's autumn time.

George Allen (9)
Parkside School

DOLPHINS

They swim through the water like a torpedo,
They glide through the air like a bird.
Above water they look like a shark,
Under, they look like the kings and queens of the ocean.
Dolphins are my favourite underwater animal
And should be free and not kept in captivity.
They should be with each other.

Oliver Bailey (10)
Parkside School

SEA STORM

Flash! Crack! The storm raged on,
Smash, clash, swaying the boat violently,
Lashing, snarling, crashing, bashing,
The swaying boat like a feather in a tornado.

Bang, crash, lash, the boat snapped in two.
Rash, crack, spark, the bolt went bang.
The lights went down
And the ship made a groaning sound.

Whoopee, the storm was over, the bay was wrecked.
The doors were bent, stuck, but we were safe,
The lifeboat was here and no storm to stop it.

Nicky Jillings (10)
Parkside School

SCARECROW

S   cary vultures pick flesh off their bodies,
C   reepy sounds are heard from the zombies,
A   rgumentative vultures fight for a skeleton to eat,
R   oaring fire surrounds the picked figures,
E   verywhere there is desolation,
C   rows circle the black, stormy sky,
R   ipped clothes cover bleached bones,
O   ver their heads the sky is ready to pour,
W   heezing bodies hang . . .

Alex Fletcher (10)
Parkside School

PETS, PETS

Pets are cute, pets are fun,
Pets are the kind that lick your thumb.

Pets, they beg for lots of food,
If you don't give it to them, they're in a bad mood.

Dog or cat you can take for a walk,
If you get a parrot, teach it to talk.

Some get happy and they swim,
Some that are abandoned lay down in sin.

People who save them are very kind,
They get new homes away from this crime.

We all know that they'll come to an end,
But till that day we'll stay as their friend.

Tom Hancock (9)
Parkside School

TROUBLE

I always get into trouble,
The next class I have to do double.
Trouble is my middle name,
Sometimes I'm a real pain.
The teachers send me out in the cold,
I stand and think about what I was told.
Most of the time I mess about,
But I'm trying hard, so please don't shout!

Kaleem Ali Khan (10)
Parkside School

MY PETS

Small, big, furry, cuddly,
Sleepy, lazy, purry, naughty.
Basil and Sybil! My kittens.
Big, cuddly, fast, naughty, stompy,
My horse, Blue!

My pets are superb, they live in my house,
But Blue lives in a stable
With wooden doors and hay on the walls.
When my cats live at home, they slouch
Around on my bunk-bed,
And that's my pets!

Felix Smith (10)
Parkside School

THE STORM

Thunder, lightning, crash! Flash! Smash!
Snarling, lashing, clash! Bash! Dash!
Twirling tornadoes coming fast,
Tidal waves, so run fast!

Tidal waves come crashing down,
Twirling tornadoes whip them round,
Thunder and lightning, man that's loud,
Watch out for that big, black cloud!

Lloyd Johns (9)
Parkside School

MY DOG

Every morning he jumps on me and licks my ears,
Especially in the night. I wake up dozily
And I see my dog, I cuddle him,
Then he nibbles me on the nose!

I take him for a walk, then suddenly he stops!
I try to drag him, but he still does not walk.
So, in the end he wins. I pick him up and say,
'Let's go home to bed!'

Raphael Leon (9)
Parkside School

THE HOUND

Staring red eyes shine in the dark,
Silk-black skin,
White teeth trickling with blood.

Guarding his territory on top of
The clouded range,
Ebony and cold as he stands.

Gravestones, fire and brimstone
Are banished and all is still
As he waits to attack!

Matthew Clark (9)
Parkside School

SCHOOL!

My day begins with a bang and a crash,
I think about my day ahead.
I think about those terrible times
When I'm sent to the deputy head.

'It's time for school!'
My mum will shout.
I reply,
'Can't I muck about?'

In music,
We have so much fun,
That afterwards,
I feel like a nun!

'It's time for lunch!
People say.
I will say,
'I'm wasting away!'

'It's time to go home,'
I will say,
Now I'm the
Only one wasting away!

Robert McManus (10)
Parkside School

A RACING CAR

A racing car is fast and smooth,
It's also very streamlined.
Its wheels whirl at the speed of light,
They can't always be timed.

Think of this car as a falcon,
Swooping for its prey
And if you want to see this car,
Come to our stadium today.

Daniel Kitcatt (10)
Parkside School

THE STORMY STORM

The trees waving their arms,
Brandishing their branches
They howl, howl like a dog,
Like prisoners in a dungeon,
They're the trees in a stormy storm

The wind spreading its hair,
Making you gasp with amazement,
The wind picking up anything in its path,
Like a hungry beggar on the streets,
This is the wind of a stormy storm.

The rain hailing on your door,
Waiting for a chance to invade,
Invade the warmth of your silent home,
Like bees swarming in a group,
This is the rain of a stormy storm.

The lightning streaking down,
Like the ship of the Devil's tail,
Escaping from the darkness,
Only for a second until swallowed up,
This is the lightning of a stormy storm.

Patrick Harman (11)
Parkside School

THE STORM

The storm came into the village,
The wind was as fast as a Formula 1 car,
Tiles were flying of the roofs of houses,
It was raining so hard, it was as if there was a big bucket
In the sky, pouring water down on our village.

I could see the sea from my bedroom window,
There were some gigantic waves,
The boats were toppling over at the port.
The wind was howling,
I thought this storm would never end.

A great roar of thunder split open the sky,
Then out of the blackness came a bolt of lightning,
Hitting a tree on its way to the ground.

Michael Fregnani (9)
Parkside School

MY DOG

My dog is playful, my dog is cute,
My dog is hairy, my dog is dirty.
She is very fast.

My dog is called Honey.
Sometimes she can be very funny.
Honey, Dad and I wrestle together,
She can be tough, though she chases a feather.

I love my dog,
And I can recognise her in the deepest fog.

Faris Toosy (9)
Parkside School

THE MAGICAL CART

A car is not just a car,
It is a magical cart with no horses.
It can speed to any destination in no time at all.
It is as fast as a runner running cross-country.
It soars to the moon like a thrown javelin,
Though sadly, it is treated very badly.
Why is it like this?
Never low on power, it puts every effort in,
Squeezing every juice of petrol to run to and fro.
Time is moving on, technologists are creating better mobiles.
The car is out of date now, it is a thing of the past!

Tristan James-Weed (11)
Parkside School

MY PET

When I got up in the morning,
I found my cat at the end of the bed,
All nice and warm, snuggled in,
With a sleepy look in his eyes.
He's cute like that.

With the teddies above him,
He glows like the sun
With heat coming off him,
Like a fire lighting the room.

I tucked him in, it felt like I
Was touching the sun.
I left him in peace with his happy dreams.
I closed the door softly and went downstairs.

Freddie Campbell (9)
Parkside School

SPRING IS BEAUTIFUL

When spring arrives, flowers come out, they are so beautiful.
In the light you see the river and fishes swimming happily
And when you look at the sky, you see the birds.
They sing their songs and are full of joy.
In the trees, you see the squirrels hiding their nuts.

James Oakley (9)
Parkside School

THE HOUND

Eyes shining in the darkness,
Teeth gleaming in the moonlight,
Hind legs as tense as mahogany,
He guards his territory.
He stands ready to pounce!

Adam Bodini (10)
Parkside School

DOLPHINS

Dolphins are joyful and love playing with people.
Cute and beautiful, they are lovely creatures.
They are happy and have sparkly, dark blue eyes.
They let you touch their delicate skin.
They love gliding beside you,
Their smooth bodies soar through the clean, cool air.

Paul Custance (10)
Parkside School

DOLPHINS

Their streamlined shape is used
To power their way through the silky sheet of ocean.
They take flight like an eagle when it sees its prey,
They blow magical water out of their blowholes,
Like a mystic fountain gives out its miracle water.
Their magnificent way of catching their prey,
Their incredible smiles light up everybody's day.

Jack Worsley (10)
Parkside School

THE HOUND

Eyes as red as blood,
Flesh-ripping teeth,
Bones marrowless and blood cold,
Silky-black fur ripples in the wind,
He hunts on a brooding, sinister night.

Brian Rud (10)
Parkside School

THE DOLPHIN

The dolphin is friendly, streamlined and cute,
Clever and high-spirited too.
The dolphin glides joyfully through the sea.

It catches its prey as fast as lightning.
It is friendly with man
And has the spirit of freedom.

Edward Kesterton (9)
Parkside School

SCARECROW

S   cary figures on sticks,
C   aring not what gruesome things they do,
A   vision of fear.
R   ipping off their skin,
E   ven snapping their brittle bones,
C   riminals to crows,
R   ising from the dead,
O   utlawed from their grave,
W   here their peaceful rest was interrupted.

Jason Porter (10)
Parkside School

THE SCARECROW

S   tanding all alone,
C   arefully guarding his crops,
A   lmost dead, yet seemingly alive,
R   arely blessed with company,
E   ver solitary,
C   reepy eyes shining,
R   agged clothes hanging limp,
O   verhead the crows circle,
W   aiting for his watchful eye to close.

Josh Smith (10)
Parkside School

SCARECROWS

Desolately standing in a field,
Eyes shining in the dark,
Clothes hanging loosely in the wind,
Crows taking no notice,
Bodies casting sinister shadows.

Skeletal frames on sticks,
Gaunt faces, not uttering a word,
Mind full of hatred and anger,
Isolated from the world.

Thomas Maddin (10)
Parkside School

SCARY SCARECROWS

S   haking figures of the night,
C   reepy noises from their gaping mouths,
A   live but dead,
R   oaring words at . . .
E   erie shadows of the night,
C   alling for drops of blood,
R   isen from the dead,
O   ften searching through the night,
W   allowing shadows of darkness,
S   ilhouetted in the darkness.

Toby Tarrant (10)
Parkside School

IN WINTER

My mum never told
Winter days are white and cold,
You will never get a tan.
We are making a snowman.
All the animals hibernate.
At this time, I stay up late.
Winter is not very long,
Singing a lot of Christmas songs.

Stefan Malakouti (11)
Parkside School

WINTER STORM

It was a windy and cold night,
The breeze made the trees shiver.
Their branches were stiff, frozen,
Even the people could hardly walk
Along the frozen snow, dumped on the street.

The snow seemed like white cotton in the air,
But snow is much cooler than cotton.
As the clean, white snow falls on the ground,
It quickly dissolves, like water.

The cold breeze makes the dissolved snow into ice,
But soon, the south wind will come and melt all the ice,
And instead of white cotton,
You would see a bright, sunny, spring day.

Boyan Baynov (10)
Parkside School

CARS

Cars, cars, zooming
From there to there,
From left to right,
Cars, cars, zooming,
Everybody's cars in sight.

Brum goes the engine,
Round go the wheels,
Over the bumps goes the car,
See how it feels.
Whoosh!

Sam Cannings (10)
Parkside School

I MET A FRIENDLY DOLPHIN

There was a dolphin,
A smooth, silky and streamlined dolphin.
He was clever and playful,
Like all other dolphins.
Through the water, dolphins
Swish and swash against the waves.

I just got to the enormous pool
And I saw the fabulous dolphin.
The man was trying to train the dolphin,
The moves that it had learnt from
The man's language were absolutely incredible.
How I would love to visit them again.

Ben Mahne (10)
Parkside School

DOLPHINS

Dolphins are as cute as anything.
Oh dolphins, how beautiful and graceful they are.
They live in the sea and all they ever eat is
Fish, fish, oh lovely fish.
Dolphins are as tame as anything,
So don't be afraid.
They glide along the surface of the waves.
Dolphins are playful, they'll play with anyone.
Their sharp teeth and smooth skin,
That's how I remember them.

Max Strait (10)
Parkside School

DOLPHINS

As dolphins glide through the water,
They leap in the air,
The clear, crystal water flies back over their heads,
Their white, sparkling teeth in their narrow mouths
Trapping fish in the space it's got,
The blowhole spraying water in the air,
Swimming smoothly in the placid ocean,
Splashing all through the fun day,
Swooping high out of the water.

Alex Davies (11)
Parkside School

MY PUPPY

My puppy is cuddly and playful,
Hairy and cute too.
He jumps on the sofa
And gives me a hug
And licks me all day and night.
He is stinky and smelly and sleeps all the time,
He eats like a pig and is as fat as a donkey.
First he goes in the mud,
Then he runs into the house.
But he is my dog
And I *love* him.

Sam Thomson (9)
Parkside School

MY PET

She's hairy and stinky, she always sleeps,
She always sneaks a bite at me.
When no one's looking, she jumps up and licks the food.
When she goes out for a walk, the first place she goes is to the mud,
She eats like a pig and is as fat as a badger.

She prowls around the house seeing what is happening,
She has her chair in the office,
She always sleeps in it.
If anyone sits there she will *bite* them.
When people ride horses by, she will always bark.
She goes crazy sometimes, like a Formula 1 driver.

Robbie Tyrrell (9)
Parkside School

MY PET

My pet is furry and purry,
Sometimes she nibbles my hat
And she leaves hair everywhere,
And guess what? She is a cat.
Sometimes she can be naughty and bite me with her jaws,
Or sometimes even scratch me with her sharp paws.
She can be useful for some things,
Like the leftover broccoli on my table plate,
I throw it under the table and she nibbles it in a state.

Richard Edkins (10)
Parkside School

THE STORM

The bright flash of lightning piercing the sky,
The amplified *boom* echoing like a wave,
And as soon as the last deafening *bang* was over,
Another arrived like a rhythmic drum,
Scarring the night sky with its blinding flash,
The rain striking the ground.
Then there's a flash and the dark night sky
Lights up for miles around,
Then just as the storm's beginning to die down,
Another ferocious lightning bolt attacks the sky,
The wind howling like a hungry wolf on the hunt,
Trees bowing and swaying in the wind against their will,
Twigs and branches cracking like a whip.
Then as if by magic, the storm ceases,
The wind stops and the rain ceases to a light drizzle.
The sun breaks out and the grass starts steaming.

Nathan Weiss (11)
Parkside School

MY CAT

My pet, we call him Cat, just Cat,
But my sister calls him Fat.
I tried to reason with her by saying he's not fat,
But she replied he is, he is fat.
We wash Cat once a year
And all he does is nothing.
My mum tried to sell him for one pound,
But still nobody took him.
Cat, he's dirty and smells of the sewers,
But I still love him and that matters.

Luke Simon (9)
Parkside School

DON'T GO OUTSIDE

Flaming fires and fearsome trees,
Mysterious wonders from lakes and seas.
Branches snapping off their trees,
Don't go outside with all the rustling leaves.

Cats lying safe in the house by the fire,
The wind whistling like a baby crier,
All you hear is miraculous sounds,
Don't go outside, it's out of bounds.

Cars outside sliding and crashing,
Famous statues breaking and smashing,
Crops in the field getting struck by blinding lightning,
All the little children staying inside, because it's too frightening.

Sam Allan (11)
Parkside School

THE GIRAFFE

Tall and elegant stands the giraffe,
Watching him eat makes me laugh.
He stretches his neck to the top of the trees,
Or spreads his legs from toes to knees
To pick up the food on the dusty ground,
Bending his neck for food he has found.
He is yellow-orange with brown spots,
His lovely long face has lots of dots.
The eyes are so big and look at you straight,
But still he's locked behind a gate!

Matthew Whelan (10)
Parkside School

STORM IN THE SKY

A blast of light flickers in the black sky,
Cracks break through the walls in the sky,
Mystery holds all who look up into the light,
As it was there and now has gone,
Seconds pass like minutes as the noise starts to rise.

All around the spirits come to shout,
Seconds they are there, but then they are gone.
The light looked harmless in the sky, but it was deadly.

The flames of revenge start to light,
A silent threat begins to rise,
A moment later they are still there.
Will the flames ever go?
Scattered liquid diamonds hit the flames,
But nothing has been done.

The sky masters begin to weep as the lonely wood
Disappears into the black soot of death.
Masters of flight never will have a home again in the wood.
Why the sky attacked its own friends we will never know.

The wind begins to rise,
The flames stand strong but grow smaller, like a piece of food,
The night begins to stare helplessly at the ground,
The sky has raged like a dog and must rest.
The storm disappears, waiting to be called back.

William Davies (11)
Parkside School

MY NAME IS ANDY

My name is Andy
And I like candy.
I get home and eat
My favourite treat.

My name is Andy,
I like to run
Around the garden in the sun,
I'm having fun.

Andy Billman (9)
Parkside School

FEAR OF THE RIVER

Speeding down the river, my mouth and nose
Clogged with water,
I am tossed and turned.
The water's current is too strong.

Being swirled and sucked under,
I gasp for breath,
But as I go faster and faster,
I notice the beauty of it all.

The glinting river ripples
As it swiftly pulls me down.
It is so powerful, but
Below the raging surface it seems quiet and calm.

I keep on looking at the birds flying above,
The river glistening, glittering from the sun,
But I realise I no longer see,
The current is pulling me under.

The gloomy depths surround me,
I cannot hear the river,
I cannot see the sky,
I float towards the light ahead.

William Patrick (10)
Parkside School

THE STORM

Flashing, crashing, lightning and thunder,
Fists of wind punching the sky,
Howling like a dog.
Rain bulleting down,
Clattering on the ground,
Falling trees, fields flooding,
People are at risk.

Escaping from the storm, people go inside
To warm up from the cold by the heat of a fire.
They listen to the rain trying to invade,
Only glass between them.

The sea is rough and waves are high,
Boats are scarce
And terrified sailors do their best
To stay afloat as breakers scrub the decks above them.
Exhausted, they sleep,
Trusting in machine and God,
They wake to a gleaming ship.
Dawn brings the calm,
Low light shimmers across a flat expanse,
Engines drone on into the distance.

Tom Bomford (11)
Parkside School

THE EVIL ELVES

They have huge, long ears
And no fears.
They are very small
And they hate to crawl.
They have lots of tricks,
They make homes with sticks.

Making mischief all day long,
They do not know they are wrong.
Evil elves are really bad,
And if you make friends, you'll be sad,
Because you, yourself,
Will become an evil elf!

Tristan Pertwee (9)
Parkside School

STORM

Flashing, crashing,
Thunderous *bang*,
Horses race towards you.

Electrifying, terrifying,
Exciting, loud,
An icy hand runs down your back.

Roaring, rolling,
Tingling, spine-chilling,
Brightness all around you.

Mystic, mysterious,
Gigantic, bright,
A booming voice rings out.

A golden sword stabs through the darkness,
Everyone is joyful,
The evil has been vanquished,
Until the next storm.

James Rowntree (11)
Parkside School

SEA STORM

The waves crash fiercely onto the cliffs,
The lightning breaks holes like a burrowing badger,
The rain pounds the frothy surface.

The thunder rumbles, shattering the calm,
Lightning lights up lots of land,
Searching, striking, killing.

Thunder amplifies and shakes the ground,
Clouds shoot out angels of death, bullets from heaven,
Striking the earth without mercy, trees fall and power lines.

The fish scatter their shoals
To find shelter from the ear-splitting sounds,
Mist covers up the howling moon,
Treetops topple, taking traces of wildlife.

A fork of lightning stabs down.
The wind screams defiance to the Earth
And a house is no more than ruins.

Bullets of rain whip up the waves, making the seas fight fiercely,
Lightning crashes, making avalanches from cliffs,
Destroying homes, devastating, dying.

The killing clouds part, then depart,
And the sea is calm again.

Ben Dunjay (11)
Parkside School

MY PET

My pet lives in a shed,
He is a funny-coloured red.
When the birds are ready to be fed,
He runs down and eats the bread.

My pet's name is Fred,
He likes to sleep on my bed.
He has a huge, ugly head,
But I love my pet named Fred.

James Watts (10)
Parkside School

THE RIPPLING RIVER

The rippling river,
Gliding like a stream of liquid silk,
Flowing freely over the riverbed.

The strong current,
Sucking like a vacuum cleaner,
Vigorously pulling procrastinating fishes down the watercourse.

The raging rapids,
Smashing down on innocent rocks and branches like a bully,
Effectively forcing them down the waterway.

The beautiful flowers,
Gazing at their reflection in the water like vain princesses,
Hanging mournfully over the edge of the weir as if weeping.

The ancient trees,
Looking over the flow of water like a father,
Looming luminously under a night sky, over the running river.

The darting fishes,
Speedily hurrying down the waterway as if something were
chasing them,
Rushing rapidly and surfing the rippling river.

Chris Douse (10)
Parkside School

WAVES

The waves clumsily came
Crashing and crumbling
Down.

The wind whipping the
Waves high into the
Air.

The sun swiftly shining
Its smooth rays along the
Waves.

The waves' ripples
Rushing rapidly to the
Seashore.

The dolphin powerfully pushing
And pulling itself over the
Waves.

Max Thomas (10)
Parkside School

THE STORM

The water was pristine clear
Before the storm,
The birds whispered in my ear,
Suddenly,
It all ended.
It was silent, silent as a lion about to pounce,
Then it stroked,
Its roar was amplifying,
The breath of the blowing of the wind
Trickled down my spine.

The forest trees falling, falling like a rock,
The clashing rocks clashed like two cymbals,
Ships disappeared in the fog,
People despair.
The Devil had come and gone,
But he was angrier,
Houses collapsed like falling trees,
All that was left was disruption and death.

Antoine Doyen (11)
Parkside School

MY FISH RODGER

Every day Rodger darts from the sea floor,
Looking for food.
He must have more.

Amazingly enough, he survives
Under the ice,
From the food that I provide.

In the summer,
He hides from the heat
To dive down low,
Into the deep,

But along comes an enormous fish
And eats up Rodger,
My fish, he's dead.

Joshua Waite (11)
Parkside School

THE MERMAID

Out in the sea,
Among the waves,
Lay the mermaid,
Resting on a rock.

Swimming all day long,
Swimming speedily through the swirling waves,
Twirling in the shimmering waters,
Her tail filled with spots.

The mermaid's pearl earrings
Glinting in the sun's rays,
Her dazzling teeth shine,
The waters sparkling in the sun.

A tanker came along,
The mermaid disappeared,
Drowning her whole existence,
The rock left empty.

James Marsh (10)
Parkside School

THE PREDATORY RIVER

The silky shine
Is blinding me,
It's flowing fast,
Gushing past the trees.

The children watch
The river rise,
Eating bushes
In its stride.

Boats are churning
Upside down,
Sailors watching
Their world go by.

The river darts by,
Swift and sure,
Swirling and whirling
For evermore.

Andrew Wynd (10)
Parkside School

THE STORM

Death-defying as it may be,
Exhilarating as it can be,
It will be as much as it should be.

Speakers amplify the noise.
If you climb on a mountain peak,
You will see it from the opposite side
Of the intergalactic universe.

You will hear it from the other side
Of the unknown part of our galaxy.
It will strike you down
Quicker than your blink.

It will strike you down
Faster than the speed of light,
The cloud is a leather jacket,
The lightning rips it with a knife,
Penetrating as deep as it can go.

Joel Ferree (11)
Parkside School

MY DOG

When my dog sees food,
He wags his tail happily.
He likes to act the fool
And is part of our family.

He likes to chew things
And he pulls things too.
He also sings
With me and you.

My dog is white,
He loves sweets that are fizzy
And he play-fights,
Which makes me dizzy.

Alex Shoult (9)
Parkside School

THE PLANET MARS

On the planet Mars,
There are lots of Martians.
Every step they take
Is enough to kill a snake.
When the snake is dead,
They put mustard in his head.
When the mustard dries,
They put diamonds in his eyes.
When the deed is done,
It is 1941!

Omer Khalid (10)
Parkside School

FOOTBALL

My favourite game in the whole world
Is football, football, football.
I play as keeper for my team,
We sometimes fight and scream.
We get sent off,
Sometimes we cough,
But we always carry on
Until the job is done.
We never give up,
'Til our team wins the cup.

Tony Humphries (10)
Parkside School

A PILOT

I've always wanted to be a pilot,
To float like a feather,
To fly like a bird,
To spend my days
Up with the sun's rays.
Now I think I can make it,
Although I'm only five,
I feel quite alive.
I can't wait to fly
High up in the sky.

Sebastian Smith (10)
Parkside School

THE RUSHING RAPIDS

The rippling, rushing rapids of the river
Suck everything in their path.
The fish try to fight, but cannot succeed
And giving up to the rapid running of the river
Are carried away, rapidly away,
From the rushing, whooshing water.

The rushing rapids are swollen by the rains,
Forcing the icy liquid to spill over banks into fields,
Covering the land around.
It's growing fiercer and stronger now than ever;
Stay well away,
For if you slip and tumble,
To fall into is control,
You will be carried away.
Your cries of help
To be drowned with you.

Ryan Threlfall (10)
Parkside School

THE MOON

The moon is glistening high above,
It comes out at night.
It is the king of the bright sky
And guides us back to our home, sweet home.
It likes to see us home from work,
A trusty friend to help you.
It cares for the Earth like it was its child,
But when it's time to go, he gives a sigh
And says 'bye' to the bright sky.

Timmy Page (9)
Parkside School

THE RAGING RIVER

The river was raging
Like an angry buckaroo.
The white water rapids
Were shimmering and blue.

The river was rushing,
Like a crowd of people.
The fishes' tails were darting and pointy,
Like a church tower's steeple.

The river was whipping
Like an excited dog's tail.
The river, unlike the sea,
Houses no whales.

Jamie Sanchez (10)
Parkside School

MY FAVOURITE PLACE

My favourite place is the beach where crabs play,
They run around sideways, so I think they're OK.
I like to make sandcastles and play in the sea,
But when it comes to ice creams, I shout, 'Yippee!'

Then it is sunset and everyone goes home
And now I'm really sad and I start to moan.
But when it comes to morning and we go down to the sea,
I start to run around - this is where I love to be.

Edward Harris (10)
Parkside School

YOUR LIFE

Brought by a stork in a bundle of cloth,
Or maybe by fairies in a cradle of moss,
You're a baby, held in your mother's hands,
Everyone staring, have you got fans?
You grow up to be a bright, smart child,
Running around being wild,
Skidding across the sandy beach.
Oh why do teachers have to teach?
Then you go to college, getting smarter and wiser,
Walking along, your best friend beside you.
All you can think of is bubblegum and sweets,
Chocolate, jelly, lots of treats,
Then someone appears, someone you love.
Where did they come from? They came from above.
Then you get married, with lots of kisses,
Accepting happily everyone's wishes.
As you get older, with a job and two kids,
Making pots of jam with sticky lids.
You're getting older, you feel it yourself,
Taxes, rent, insurance - your health.
Then you're a granny, no longer young,
With wrinkles on your knees, forehead and tongue.
You've had a very good life, you're eighty-seven,
Now the day's come to go up to Heaven.

Sophie Hughes (9)
Reigate Priory Junior School

UNTITLED

I'm travelling to visit my mum in hospital.
They think she's got cancer.
I'm so scared that she won't recognise me,
I'm scared of the way she will look as well.

I really want to help,
To make her completely better.
I know I can't do anything,
I feel so inconspicuous.

I feel like I'm not in my body,
I'm away on a distant planet.
A lump swells up inside my throat,
I struggle to keep it in.

A tear dribbles down my face,
I don't bother to brush it away.
I only hear my thoughts,
As they fret inside my skull.

Whatever happens, I will do my best.
I will never give up until she dies.
I will never forgive myself for all the times when
                             I have annoyed her,
I should have been good. I should. I should.

Sam Hyams (10)
Reigate Priory Junior School

THE JOURNEY THROUGH TIME

It is now 2001,
The world has barely begun.

The future, 3023,
It will definitely be in a new century.

There will, of course, be flying cars,
The scientists' brains would have gone bizarre.

We will definitely be living in space,
There will be more of the human race.

We will be talking to the animals,
Our new sport will be bowls with cannon balls.

But it is still 2001,
And none of this has yet begun.

Katie Shearman & Eleanor Hutchinson (9)
Reigate Priory Junior School

A PANTHER'S LIFE

Panther, panther, crawls so low,
Watching all the monkeys as they come and go.
Panther, panther, hunts for food,
I do not know why he's in a mood.
Panther, panther, goes way to play,
He's playing his games,
Hunting the hunter,
Poaching the poacher,
Scouting the scouts.
Panther, panther, is now asleep,
In the morning, he will find you to eat.

Joe Vines (8)
Reigate Priory Junior School

JOURNEY OF AN E-MAIL

Pedestrian e-mails, e-mails with wings,
E-mails with wheels and turbines and things.

As fast as a thought, a boat for its port
And lawful as ever, a judge in a court.

As sharp as a wild cat, wearing a top hat,
And boring as the sentence, 'sat on a mat'.

The quizzical e-mail sets off on its sail,
Whirring and bleeping, leaving its trail.

It speeds through the cybernet, whizzing and blasting,
But only the e-mail stays everlasting.

Cole Lilley (10)
Reigate Priory Junior School

THE MONKEY

With power, through the trees he goes,
The monkey's soft fur blows and blows.
Above some thorns a monkey lurks,
You hear the chattering, the gibbering.

In a flash, the monkey's swinging away,
He sees an oak where he lands safely,
The cheeky humour,
The bananas reach his mouth.

He sees a branch,
He jumps up there.
So beware, watch out,
The monkey could be about!

Matthew Walker (9)
Reigate Priory Junior School

NAN AND GRANDDAD

My nan and granddad
Sit and walk.
They're like birds with broken wings,
Generous as rich magicians,
Playing games, that's their game.
They're never sad like an old, foggy day,
Sit in front of the fire,
They do it most days.
Granddad burns paper with a magnifying glass,
Nan's in her room, working on the computer.
They're the best.

Kay Edwards (9)
Reigate Priory Junior School

I CAN

I can creep,
I can crawl,
I can dash,
I can bolt,
I can run,
I can jog,
I can tiptoe,
I can strut,
I can sprint,
I can slide,
I can walk,
I can,
I can,
I can *move.*

Chelsea Hiley (8)
Reigate Priory Junior School

JOURNEY OF AN E-MAIL

The claw-like fingers rapidly type on the trembling keyboard.
The shuddering mouse selects 'send.'
Screech of it goes travelling through the airways,
Dodging and swerving through the air traffic.
Suddenly it drops at an unbelievable rate,
Still with its cautions not to overpower and crash.
It's safe and received and ready to be opened.

Matthew Butler (10)
Reigate Priory Junior School

MY FAMILY

My family is pretty weird.

My brother is a star,
Sits somewhere, not moving.

My mum is a bookworm,
Reading anything she can lay her hands on.

My nan is a chatterbox,
Chatting and chatting and chatting.

My aunts are walking lips,
Following me and giving me kisses. Yuck!

My uncles are slobs,
Eating and drinking forever more.

And me . . . I am just as bad,
I'm a soldier, fighting everyone.

Sarah Sheen (9)
St Catherine's Primary School, Bletchingley

THE MOMENT OF SILENCE

It was so silent that I heard
My mum and dad's TV in their room.

It was so peaceful that I heard
The midnight wind blow around the whole room.

It was so still that I felt
The spooks and haunts inside the horror house.

It was so silent that I heard
The birds inside the forest, whistling.

It was so quiet that I senses
My granddad in heaven smiling at me.

It was so hushed that I heard
The trees in the midnight air.

Calvin Copard (9)
St Catherine's Primary School, Bletchingley

MY MUM

My mum is as cuddly as a teddy bear,
As soft as a bed,
As bright as a light in the sky,
As clever as a teacher,
As happy as a princess,
As funny as a clown in a circus,
As slim as a twig,
As pretty as a rose,
Who loves dragons,
And finally,
She's the best mum in the world.

Emma Booth (9)
St Catherine's Primary School, Bletchingley

SILENCE

It was so silent that I heard
A woodpecker quietly pecking on the old tree outside.

It was so still that I felt
The loose strings of cotton on my duvet tickling my feet.

It was so peaceful that I heard
Some raindrops trickle down the trees' leaves.

It was so silent that I heard
Tom Ballan's tree house creaking.

It was so quiet that I sensed
My dad brushing his teeth in the bathroom.

It was so hushed that I heard
A house martin tweaking the twigs in his nest.

Ben Dawson (9)
St Catherine's Primary School, Bletchingley

THERE'S SOMETHING UP IN THE ATTIC

There's something up in the attic,
I saw it and went into a panic!
But I did not let it show,
Because he had eyes that were all aglow.
He looked cuddly, until I saw those jaws,
Which were very scary
And hairy,
And those great, enormous claws!

Harriet Plummer (9)
St Catherine's Primary School, Bletchingley

My Bedroom Is

My bedroom is a dump,
With piles and piles of unknown things,
Toxic waste that no one should touch.

My bedroom is a minefield,
It is a dinosaur graveyard,
As large as the universe.

My bedroom is a lost city waiting to be discovered,
It is as dangerous as a lion's den,
That's why people enter at their own risk!

Stewart Wilson (9)
St Catherine's Primary School, Bletchingley

I Saw A Battle!

I saw a battle,
It was big, it was.
There were lots of ships
And the planes kept making a rattle.
There were guns and bombs
From the American soldiers.

I saw a war,
It was massive.
There were Indians,
With swords and claws.
There were cannons and tanks
From the Americans
To blow them all to
Kingdom come!

Andrew Boutle (10)
St Catherine's Primary School, Bletchingley

MY MUM

My mum is a cream leather sofa,
Her laugh is bouncy,
She keeps clear of trouble.
She is as expensive as
A sofa in Buckingham Palace.

My mum is as strong as a knight,
If she saw a dragon, she would
Spin it around and around,
And then would stop.
She is a heroine - one of a kind.

Sam Kempton (10)
St Catherine's Primary School, Bletchingley

THE SUN IS A?

The sun is a red Smartie,
With fiery 'E' numbers.

The sun is a golden leaf,
Blowing in the wind.

The sun is a button on my shirt
I need to sew back on,

The sun is a buttercup,
Floating in a puddle.

The sun is half a slice of cake.
The sun is setting,
Now, it's gone.

Danielle Puleston (9)
St Catherine's Primary School, Bletchingley

NANNA'S ROAST

I can smell the dinner,
I think it's . . .
Roast!
The Yorkshire pudding makes me faint,
The thick gravy,
The thick sliced carrots, yum.
You should see how much juicy chicken I get,
It's lovely.
I wish my brother was the chicken,
Because he's fat and I would be eating all night.

Sam Kelly (9)
St Catherine's Primary School, Bletchingley

MY FAMILY

My sister is a shark,
Very vicious and fast.
She hangs around the wildlife park,
But she's always last.

My brother is a dragon,
He makes me rather scared.
I know I'll never be killed by him
Because I know he really cares.

My other sister is a rabbit,
She follows me everywhere.
She has lots of habits,
But she goes anywhere.

Emily Field (10)
St Catherine's Primary School, Bletchingley

PEACE AND QUIET

It was so silent that I heard the wind whistling
Where the trees were banging against it.

It was so peaceful that I heard my sister
Breathing down below me.

It was so silent that I heard my cat's
Tiptoes coming up the stairs.

It was so quiet that I sensed
Someone coming in the window.

It was so hushed that I heard my cat
Get into bed with my little sister.

Kayleigh Morewood (8)
St Catherine's Primary School, Bletchingley

I KNOW WHERE THE TEACHERS GO

The teachers go to the marking shop,
To get the work marked.
While they are waiting,
They go to the teachers' bar
And have a glass of red wine.
They go to the desk shop
To buy a desk.
They go back to the marking shop
To collect the work.
They go home.
Is this true?

Shane Drayton (10)
St Catherine's Primary School, Bletchingley

THE WIND

The wind, the wind, is like a devil,
Crashing through the trees,
Pushing poor little children over,
Like a horrid bully teasing them,
Then they fall and hurt themselves,
Quite badly.

The wind, the wind, is like an angel,
Floating gracefully through the trees,
Cooling the hot and bothered,
Like a fan on hot summer days,
As they drink their cold drinks
And lick their lollipops.

Victoria Crowe (9)
St Catherine's Primary School, Bletchingley

ROASTIE

One shouting turkey,
Two squeaking lambs,
Three running runner beans,
Four Martian sprouts,
Five furry potatoes,
Six flapping chickens,
Seven pigs beheaded,
Eight peacocks sent to England.

Let's mix it all up –
Yummy!

David Bailey (10)
St Catherine's Primary School, Bletchingley

MILKY WAY

The sun shining brightly is a flickering one pound coin,
Mercury is a crackling oven, *pop!*
Venus is a suffocating gas ball, no oxygen to breathe.
Earth is a planet spinning automatically,
Mars is a red marble rolling across a stone floor,
Jupiter is a giant red beach ball, thrown up from Hell!
Saturn is a giant cheeseburger with cheese dripping out!
Uranus is a coral reef with bright turquoise water,
Neptune is a deep blue sea with giant crashing waves,
Pluto is a huge golf ball putted down from Heaven!

Lawrence McSheen (10)
St Catherine's Primary School, Bletchingley

OUR FUTURE

I want a world where
The world cares for others,
To recycle, not waste!
Put rubbish in the bin, not on the floor,
War is no more,
Children respect adults,
Where tolerance is good.

I want a world where
We help others,
No horrible future,
People living in harmony,
Help to do the homework,
Where kindness is forever.

I will start changing *me!*

Katie Whitwick (10)
St Catherine's Primary School, Bletchingley

IN THE WAR

The people in the war
Are as brave as hyenas,
Sitting in their trenches,
In pain.

The people in the war
Are shooting off their guns,
Limping in the mud,
In pain.

The people in the war
Are fighting for the country,
Saving other people,
In pain.

The people in the war
Are laughing and joking,
For winning the war,
In pain.

Christopher Ward-Morris (10)
St Catherine's Primary School, Bletchingley

THE SEA

The sea is a blob of ink,
The sea is water in a huge sink,
It's the sky on the ground,
It's a huge swimming pool,
It's a wavy street,
Blue paint from a tub,
Soggy blue paper,
A huge tub of water.

Nicholas Clements (10)
St Catherine's Primary School, Bletchingley

I WANT TO BUILD A WORLD WHERE

I want to build a world where
Terrorism is no more,
Where ignorance is dead
And understanding is all.

I want to build a world where
Children respect their parents,
Where kindness and forgiveness thrive
And intolerance has no place.

I will start by changing small things,
I will start with me.
Be better at school and
Help my friends with work.

Ricky King (11)
St Catherine's Primary School, Bletchingley

ANOTHER WORLD

Fireballs plummeting down
From the mouths of the fire horses of death.
Spectacular sparks soaring into space
Belonging to the scalding pits of Hell.
A belching lava demon propelling large quantities of lava,
Its revolting stench from its maw
Polluting the air.
Swirling through time
Until the sun burns out,
Like a rip in space
Which is a never-ending vortex.

Chloe Phipps (10)
St Catherine's Primary School, Bletchingley

OUR FUTURE

Tolerance shall change the world,
But only if you tolerate good, never bad.

We shall be more mature to other people
And act like ladies and gentlemen.

We must be happy, but without playing jokes on other people,
Laugh with your friends, make them smile.

We shall get kinder, help old people across road,
Don't pull hair on playgrounds.

Don't forget to be religious, doesn't matter what your colour,
Behave as your religion.

We shall make peace across the world,
No war shall occur, peace forever.

Corsica Harrison-Lyons (10)
St Catherine's Primary School, Bletchingley

HELL IS LIKE

Hell is like a fiery place with toxic fumes,
Lava that melts, scorching hot,
Endless corridors with empty rooms,
A mother whose baby's been stolen from its cot.

People screaming - all the time,
Satan laughing on his throne,
Alleys and walkways full of crime,
Skulls and skeletons and all types of bone.

Matthew McKinney (9)
St Catherine's Primary School, Bletchingley

TRAIN OF THOUGHT

The train of thought rushed into the station,
Screeching to a sudden halt.
All aboard for platform three,
The thought of a lemon tree.
Then we're off to platform five,
The thoughts over there are spell-binding,
So all the brain cells climb aboard.
A fumbling of newspapers, a rattling of bags,
And . . . we're off!
I thought we would not make it!

Kitty Kinder (10)
St Catherine's Primary School, Bletchingley

THE BEAR

My sister is a cuddly bear,
Her hair is silky,
She's soft to touch.
She snuggles next to me
When she is cold.
I talk and play with her -
She is my friend.

My sister turned eleven,
She is now a grizzly bear.
She snaps and snarls at me,
She growls when I come near.
She's hard and rough to touch,
I don't get too close.
I wish I could find
My cuddly bear.

Rebecca Silk (9)
St Catherine's Primary School, Bletchingley

THE WORLD I WANT TO LIVE IN

I'd like to live in a world where there is
No litter on the floor,
No fighting between one another.

I'd like to live in a world where
It doesn't matter about your skin colour,
Where people live in peace.

I'd like to live in a world where
People listen to one another,
Where children respect their parents.

I'd like to live in a world where
People don't harm one another,
Don't kill each other,

So we can all live in peace.

Pamela Davies (11)
St Catherine's Primary School, Bletchingley

THE WRITER OF THIS POEM

The writer of this poem is,

As beautiful as the sunset,
As calm as the sea,
As kind as a butterfly,
As lucky as you see.

As thoughtful as my mother,
As respectful as the Pope,
As peaceful as the North Star,
As bright as a ray of hope.

Aimie Davies (10)
St Catherine's Primary School, Bletchingley

TIME TO MYSELF

It was so silent that I heard the
Rustle of papers, the sound of papers whispering to me.

It was so peaceful that I heard a snake
Hissing at me, hissing and spitting at me.

It was so still, that I felt
The sun beaming down on me, burning me.

It was so silent that I heard
The water dripping down the drain, making a tune for me.

It was so still that I felt
The sun beaming down on me.

It was so hushed that I heard
My mum thinking about shopping for dinner.

It was so quiet that I sensed
The sound of Dad's crutches clacking on the floor.

Tabitha Harrison-Lyons (8)
St Catherine's Primary School, Bletchingley

WAR

Joy is nice, war is sad,
I don't want to be a soldier.
Joy is happy, war is terror,
I don't want to be a soldier.
Joy is rest, war is death,
I don't want to be a soldier.
Joy is peace, war is guns,
I want to be at home.

Tom Ient (8)
St Catherine's Primary School, Bletchingley

MY GRANDAD WAS EVACUATED

My grandad was sent away,
He was evacuated.
It was cold,
My grandad felt scared.
He went to Wales.
When the war finished,
My great-grandad was dead,
He was killed.
My grandad said
He did not say goodbye.

Natalie Whittaker (8)
St Catherine's Primary School, Bletchingley

EVACUATED

Mum took me to the station,
Nervous children trying not to cry,
A smelly engine hissed and spat,
The train gathered speed.
We all sang a song,
Journey's end, my tears began.

Jordan Dopson (8)
St Catherine's Primary School, Bletchingley

WHO WILL PICK YOU?

It is frightening to be an evacuee.
Who will pick you,
A kind person or a bad person?
Who will pick you?
Who will?

Stephen Martins (9)
St Catherine's Primary School, Bletchingley

In The Future

Dear Three Little Pigs,

I would like the world to be more forgiving and caring,
The big, bad wolves not being so mean and selfish.
People have got to be happy, joyful and not hurt others.
In the future, I am gong to be a fireman,
So when other people are in trouble, I can help.
We should help wolves and pigs that have not homes
And help the pigs who are disabled.

Reece Cobby (11)
St Catherine's Primary School, Bletchingley

In The Future

In the future, I hope it will be a world of peace,
No nasty wars, no terrorists, no bad people,
No people dying of starvation or thirst,
No racism or bad name-calling,
In the world.

Alex Hill (11)
St Catherine's Primary School, Bletchingley

Evacuee

My friend was an evacuee,
She missed her mother, father and sister.
When the war was over,
She found her mother, father and sister,
It seemed her life had disappeared.

Carlene Egan (9)
St Catherine's Primary School, Bletchingley

MY THOUGHTS FOR THE FUTURE

I want to build a world where
Black and white are equal.
Where unhappiness is the past
And friendliness the future.

I want to build a world where
People live in harmony,
Where war will cease
And peace survive.

I want to build a world where
Terrorism is no more,
Where ignorance will die
And understanding is for all.

I want to build a world where
People respect each other,
Where kindness and forgiveness thrive
And intolerance has no place.

I will start by changing small things.
I will start with *me!*

Ryan Came-Johnson (10)
St Catherine's Primary School, Bletchingley

BATTLEFIELDS

I never wanted to be a soldier,
But I had to be.
The battlefields are full of
Bullet-riddled men,
Both German and British,
Both friend and foe.

I'll always remember my
Friends who have fallen,
Although I never wanted
To be a soldier.

Thomas Evans (8)
St Catherine's Primary School, Bletchingley

So Silently

It was so silent that I heard
The eyelids drop of a distant stranger
In a faraway land.

It was so peaceful that I heard
The spider in the shed making his web
To catch his prey.

It was so still that I felt
The silent touch of the cat leaping off the chair
As he went to bed.
It was so silent that I heard
The water dripping down the drain.

It was so quiet that I sensed
The sound of the wind
As it blew in the trees.

It was so hushed that I heard
The distant cries of someone calling for help.

Catherine Farnfield (9)
St Catherine's Primary School, Bletchingley

THOUGHTS FOR THE FUTURE

I want to build a world where
Terrorism is no more,

Where racism is dead
And harmony is for all.

I want to build a world where
Children respect their parents,

Where people of all kinds unite
And erase all evil.

I want to build a world where
Waste is the past and recycling the future,

Where war will be wiped out
And forgiveness will thrive.

I will start by trying to change small things.
I will start with me.

Christopher Mason (11)
St Catherine's Primary School, Bletchingley

WITCHES

W   itches, witches, they're horrible hags.
I   ncredibly foul smelling, obese witches.
T   erribly torturous, old and ancient.
C   auldron lovers, they like making trouble.
H   ogs' tusks, bats and owlet's wings
      that's what they put in some of their spells.
E   verybody hates them
S   pells, they think they're potion masters.

Laura Coltman (10)
Royal Alexandra & Albert School

THE FUN FAIR

I can smell doughnuts, they are fresh from the shop,
I can hear chatter like lots of sea lions barking,
I can hear music from the rides
And people screaming on the roller coaster,
I can see lights on the rides,
I can also see the big blue sea which is like a big blue balloon,
I can see seagulls when I'm on the big wheel,
I can touch the entrance bars and the queue rope,
I can taste fish 'n' chips from the chippy,
I can taste candyfloss,
I like the fair!

Jasmine Panter (10)
Royal Alexandra & Albert School

ALL ABOUT ME AS A BOARDER

I really miss my brother, mum and dad.
It makes me feel very sad.
I sat down and thought for a while
About things that make me smile.
My favourite programme is about a man
He does martial arts and his name is Jackie Chan.
I like things that are yummy
Because they do good things to your tummy.
I like food like burgers and chips
Because sometimes there are nice dips.
The drinks I like never make me choke
Like a strawberry milkshake and a glass of coke.

Marvin Trundle (10)
Royal Alexandra & Albert School

MY FRIENDS

My friends are really special,
They mean a lot to me,
Everyone is different,
Exactly how it should be.
Lotty's always chatty,
She keeps me well informed.
It makes the day go faster,
And stops me getting bored.
Frankie's always laughing,
Full of so much fun,
She's funky, cool and funny,
To me she's no. 1.
Roise's always caring,
And very good at sharing,
If I'm feeling sad or blue,
She's the one I would turn to.
Friends like these
Are worth more than gold,
A priceless treasure
That can never be sold.

Sophia Cardillo (11)
Royal Alexandra & Albert School

MANILA

There once was a man from Manila,
Who looked just like a gorilla,
He danced to Thriller
And liked vanilla
And got on so well with Godzilla.

David Perry (11)
Royal Alexandra & Albert School

STOP AND THINK

There once was a dolphin
Of a shade of blue,
It's amazing
What he can do.

Splishing and splashing
Through the curl
Of the sea, acting free.

It's horrible to think
That dolphins
Might be extinct.

If you are thinking
You want a bet
Stop . . . think,
Would you like
To be caught up
In a net?

Emily Stringer (11)
Royal Alexandra & Albert School

SUNSHINE

You're my sunshine,
You shine so brightly,
You're so gold like the sun,
Your sparkly lights are so beautiful,
You're like a golden blob in the sky,
You make the rain go away,
I love you so much,
Please don't run away.

Felicity Hartley (9)
Royal Alexandra & Albert School

CRAMPED

You, you with your huge fingers pick me up!
This rectangular object comes towards me
and all I see . . . is sparks.
Then suddenly, a hot, but beautiful, dangerous,
multicoloured flame, a raindrop upside down shape
is formed between the containers of wonders
and your wrinkly thumb.
You burn my healthy pine head.
Sssssscratch . . . my reddy-amber top is slashed
across my cramped home.
I share a cramped box between my fellow sticks.
We all wonder who you will pick,
to do your honourable task.
It is quite cramped but I suppose we all don't live long.
Oh, oh I've been chosen.
Sssssscratch . . . the fire is burning and roaring.
I gracefully burn for you.

Shadé Solomon (11)
Royal Alexandra & Albert School

IF YOU EVER

If you ever, ever, ever, ever
If you ever, ever, ever, ever met a bee
You must never, never, never, never
You must never, never, never, never touch its sting
If you ever, ever, ever, ever
If you ever, ever, ever, ever touch its sting
Never, never see another bee.

Courtney Todd (8)
Royal Alexandra & Albert School

SMUDGIE THE HAMSTER

I'm a ball of fluff, I love to run,
Swing on bars and fill my tum.
My owner's great, I'm one year old,
She always makes sure I never get cold.
I love to play in my ball all day
I'm even looked after when she's away.
I've been hurt and scared just once
By a big ugly rat,
Who was a bit of a dunce,
He hurt my friends and some did die,
I'm telling the truth, I dare not lie.
But I am loved and that I'm glad,
By now you must think I'm slightly mad!

Jemma Howell (11)
Royal Alexandra & Albert School

EVACUEES IN TERROR

The dirt and smell of oily faces
Dirt full shoes, with untied laces,
The crying so loud not to echo.

It's hard to believe what I am saying
Their hope is fading
For the lives of those children.

No shoes, dirty feet,
They would have had no meat to eat.

Packed with suitcases, the train,
Confused are their brains
Feeling scared when they come to land.

William Stringer (8)
Royal Alexandra & Albert School

MY PARENTS

My name is Hannah
I'm nine years old.
I'm gonna tell you a story
That needs to be told.

I live in a house with my mum and dad
Sometimes it's good
And sometimes it's bad.

It was a cold, wet day back in November
I went out with my mum.
It was a day to remember
My mum said, 'Hey Hannah
Let's go to a dance'
I was gonna say 'No'
But I didn't get the chance
When my mother hit the dance floor
I couldn't believe it, it was an eyesore.
So there she was jiggin' all over the place
And I just stood there
With a big red face.

The second story's about my dad.
The strangest experience
I've ever had.
A night of fun for this typical blokey
Was to take me to a bar
For some karaoke.
When we got inside
The place was packed
But when my dad got to the mic
He soon changed that.

He sang and sang
And he sang out of tune
It was so bad he emptied the room.

So that's my story
I hope you liked it,
So when you are doing something funny
Tell me, cause I'll write it.

Hannah Gomall (9)
Royal Alexandra & Albert School

THE MAGIC BOX

I will put in my box
Five golden wishes.
My treasure,
A rabbit eating,
A silver chain.

I will put in my box
My best pen,
My best pencil,
My best work.

I will lock my box in a secret cupboard,
You lock it with a key.
It's got stars and zigzags all over it,
My name is on the top.

Rushil Patel (9)
Royal Alexandra & Albert School

FOOTBALL CRAZY

I am football mad, football crazy,
When it comes to football I'm not lazy,
Whether it rains, whether there is sun,
I always play football and have some fun.
Then I played a match and got bored,
I couldn't believe how many goals they scored.
Then we came back, still 5-2,
Then we won 'cause I went on to score quite a few.

Samuel Horridge (11)
Royal Alexandra & Albert School

I AM MAGIC

I am magic, I am tall,
I am very proud to be so cool.
When I come to you will have
Four good, long, fantastic, sparkly, wicked wishes.
If not you can have magic.
Close your eyes and I'll be there
On the stroke of midnight.

Kim McDade (9)
Royal Alexandra & Albert School

HONEY

H ot, nice and sunny, blue sky
O n a hill eating honey apples
N ice, sweet, shining honey
E leven buzzing bees hungry for my honey
Y ou get the dribbling honey taste in your mouth.

Anthony Fountain (11)
Royal Alexandra & Albert School

DOLPHINS

Dolphins play in the summer sun,
They feel like rubber
And look such fun
With fins and noses and shiny teeth
They slide and splash.

I love to watch them swim along
It's where I feel they belong.

Stephanie Evans (10)
Royal Alexandra & Albert School

HORSES

H orses gallop through the fields
O ver jumps so they can win the race
R iders whip the horses to make them go faster
S addles are fitted so people can ride
E ating hay all the time
S hy do the horses when they are scared.

Paige Stewart-Thompson (10)
Royal Alexandra & Albert School

MY BEACH POEM

The water is nice and clean
A lot of people go there,
The surfers are all there
And kids are eating ice cream.
The sun is still shining and giving off heat,
But when it comes 5 o'clock
Everybody goes home to eat.

James Tuffill (10)
Royal Alexandra & Albert School

PETS AND ME

After I had learnt to crawl
Although I was still very small,
My mum went out and brought me a pet
A guinea pig, that I called Jet.

As I got bigger and learnt to walk
About the same time I started to talk,
Another guinea pig came home to stay,
And this one I called May.

By the time I went to school
I thought my pets were very cool
They had lots of babies, you see,
And they were all friends with me.

As I grow up, a dog we get,
And we all love her a lot,
Her name is Queenie, a border collie,
The person who didn't want her, must be a wally.

I brought a snake with my pocket money,
And my mum, she thinks it's very funny,
Because, for my dad, a snake is his worst hate,
But I've got it now, so it's too late.

Of all the pets that we have got,
I guess we have got rather a lot,
I think my snake's the best
But I still love all the rest.

Jack Mayle (10)
Royal Alexandra & Albert School

THE UNICORN

Shining, glistening
Like a mirror that shines in the light.
It's like a dream floating through my head.
Its neck strong and high with pride.
Its horn sharp and long like a needle.
It looks!
It's looking at me!
I don't understand,
Why doesn't it run?
It starts to walk,
Gathering speed and galloping
Then suddenly . . .
It's gone!

Charlotte Clark (10)
Royal Alexandra & Albert School

ALTERNATIVE POEM

One wicked wish
Two tiny tulips
Three tormenting tigers
Four Freaky frogs
Five filthy fossils
Six scary skeletons
Seven squishy snakes
Eight enormous elephants
Nine nasty newts
Ten talking teachers.

Zoe-Michelle Carter (11)
Royal Alexandra & Albert School

SWEETS

I love sweets,
Cola bottles fizzle
Mars Bars squish
Crunchies crunch
I can't live without them
I love the way they go down my throat
I love to lick a Creme Egg's inside
I love to think about the sugary mixture
They make me drool and slurp,
I'm driving my mum to despair
But I don't care
Because I love sweets.

George Hughes (11)
Royal Alexandra & Albert School

MY PET TODD

My pet Todd,
Is very odd.
He's got different coloured eyes
And sounds pathetic when he cries.
He's missing some toes
And has a squashed nose.
He lies on my bed all day
And at night goes out to play.
I love him lots
And he likes dots.
He hates getting wet,
But he's still my pet.

Danielle Coomber (9)
Royal Alexandra & Albert School

MAGIC BOX

I will put in my box
A warm heart from a freezing ice man,
I will put in black fire from a red volcano,
A knight's bravery,
A cobra's poison,
Speed from a rabbit,
Camouflage from a tarantula,
Sight from an eagle,
Muscles as strong as the Earth,
A leaf as sharp as a blade,
Black ice from a red lake,
The colours of day
And a life that is invincible.

Ross Carney (9)
Royal Alexandra & Albert School

MY ALLITERATIVE POEM

One wicked witch
Two tiny twins
Three terrific toys
Four fire fighters
Five funky friends
Six silly snakes
Seven singing singers
Eight eating elephants
Nine naughty netball players
Ten terrible tigers.

Komal Patel (10)
Royal Alexandra & Albert School

THE GREY SQUIRREL

The grey squirrel ran
fast up the tree.
Then it stopped
on a branch
and stared at me.

It put its paws
to its tiny face
and nibbled away.
Another squirrel came
so they had a race.

Down the tree trunk
they started to play.
Backwards and forwards and then
a car horn sounded
and they ran quickly away.

Felicity Edwards (9)
Royal Alexandra & Albert School

MY ALLITERATIVE POEM

One worthy witch
Two tricky twins
Three thin tigers
Four fishes fighting
Five filthy Ferraris
Six sizzling sausages
Seven sick septuplets
Eight elephants eating
Nine naughty nuggets
Ten talking telephones.

Rosanna Lewis (11)
Royal Alexandra & Albert School

WITCH

Up in the air
Guess what I see?
A witch with green hair
Staring at me.

What does she do,
That odd looking witch?
I stare at her too
Then she falls in a ditch.

Now covered in mud
She doesn't look scary.
With holes in her socks
I'm no longer wary.

Now I can see
With her in a mess.
She's a child of three
In fancy dress.

Lucy Stringer (10)
Royal Alexandra & Albert School

SNOWDROPS AND WINTER

Snowdrops on the trees
Snowdrops on the grass
Snowdrops on the car
Snowdrops everywhere!

Winter is so chilly
Winter is so frosty
Winter is for playing
Winter is for fun.

Ian Wylie (9)
Royal Alexandra & Albert School

ELREKI MY PET DOG

E   lreki is my special pet dog
L   oops she does in the air
R   ings she has on her special paws
E   ats a little amount of food
K   ieran my brother plays with her
I   n the house they mess about

M   y dog Elreki is so much fun
Y   ou'll love her when you see her

D   oes a lot of naughty stuff
O   bviously she is very crazy,
G   oes to bed very quietly at night.

Rebecca Wright (10)
Royal Alexandra & Albert School

NUTTER

I'm a bit of a nutter,
My house is all a clutter,
They feed me on bread,
And send me to bed.
I try to escape
But they put on my brake.
I go down to tea
And what do I see,
But it's only peanut butter
For a nutter!

Reuben Smith (9)
Royal Alexandra & Albert School

MY DOG SOPHIE

My dog Sophie
She's quite dopey.

She walks into trees
I beg on my knees
That she will never get a disease.

She walks around
Sniffing the ground
Isn't she a silly hound.

Rebekah Chaplin (10)
Royal Alexandra & Albert School

CARS

Cars are fast
Cars are slow
Cars are old
Cars are new

Cars have wheels
Cars have windows
Cars have roofs
Cars have doors

Cars are sporty
Cars are for family
Cars are big
Cars are small.

Blue Jackson (10)
Royal Alexandra & Albert School

THE EXCUSES

Never say the dog did eat your prep.
Never say a Martian took it.
Never say the house burnt down and it burnt with it.
Never say a thief came and took it.
Never say a policeman arrested it
Because the teacher will say it is a load of rubbish.
Never say your friend wanted extra prep.
Never say I was busy doing rocket science.
Never say my brother put it on a firework
Because the teacher will say, 'Try the other one.'

Rhys Gilbert (9)
Royal Alexandra & Albert School

I HAD A DREAM

I had a dream that I was an elf,
I lived in the town of Rivendell among other elves,
High in the mountains, high, high,
I listened to the tinkling of the water,
Peaceful, quiet, silence,
The flowers sparkled in the glittering light,
Sparkling, glittering in the light,
I listened to the falling water,
Falling, falling, falling.

Eleanor Rodger (10)
Royal Alexandra & Albert School

TWEETY

Tweety Pie is so sweet like apple pie
And the cat wants him to die.
I think Tweety should be called Sweety because he's so sweet.
Tweety is so kind on tests, he never will cheat.
I'd like to be Tweety, it would be cool
I wouldn't have to go to school.
But there's one bad thing, it's the cat
I wish we had a stick mat
That way the cat wouldn't come back!

Sara Harrington (9)
Royal Alexandra & Albert School

MY BEDDY TEDDY

I like beddy,
But I don't like my teddy
That is in my beddy.
Here comes Mummy
Mummy likes the teddy
That is sitting in my beddy.
Here comes Daddy!
Daddy hates the teddy
In my beddy.
Mummy, Daddy
Fight over beddy teddy.
Teddy gone!

Samantha Taylor (10)
Royal Alexandra & Albert School

LOST TREASURE

In the greedy gold box,
On the treasure trampler,
Under the wave crasher,
Lives the blood-red, deep red,
Precious diamond stones,
The treasure.

Left from the greedy takers,
Who sailed on their sea floater,
Up to the treasure trampler,
Down to the rubies and gold,
But the greedy gobblers
Foolishly died
Leaving their treasure behind.

Frances Charman (10)
Weyfield Primary School

HIDDEN TREASURE

Sand sweeper,
Padlock pouncer,
Treasure trampler,
Chain challenger,
Silver shaker,
Bronze breaker,
Gold gobbler,
Water waiter,
Shell shaker,
Stone stunner,
Wooden wounder,
Chest chaser.

Jamie Kitching (10)
Weyfield Primary School

HIDDEN TREASURE

The box sighs as it opens,
Years have passed,
Still not broken,
As the key turns the lock,
Expecting to see gold and bronze,
All it sees is a tattered book,
Falling to pieces with the stress it has took.

The contents float upwards,
Yellow with age,
Soft green moss still growing on the page,
The ink spread out,
The date not clear,
The name has almost disappeared,
Where it came from,
Nobody knows,
But it's the diary of someone long ago.

Kirsten Pady (10)
Weyfield Primary School

HIDDEN TREASURE

My treasure is hidden under the depths of the ocean,
in a dark, gloomy cave stands the treasure chest,
but warning protected
by an octoswirler.
But nearby is a sand swifter,
sand keeper hyposwirler,
sand cruncher, spirit of the dead!

Jamie Smithers (10)
Weyfield Primary School

THE HUNT

I looked.
There, over there,
It was a treasure chest,
In the bottom of the ocean,
I looked.

I looked.
What's inside it?
It was in the ocean,
It had disappeared. Where was it?
I looked.

The beach,
It's on the beach,
I tried to open it,
I found something inside it.
But what?

Elizabeth Hill (11)
Weyfield Primary School

HIDDEN TREASURE

Under the open ocean,
lays long lost treasure.

Dropped from a water
waver ship, which is now
rotting under the slimy seaweed.

The creepy captain
skeleton is guarding the bubbly
chests.

Francesca Guinchard (10)
Weyfield Primary School

WHAT AM I LOOKING FOR?

What? Why?
Dark stormy night,
What am I looking for?
Clouds are grey and rain is coming,
When? Where?

Sky mad,
Heavens, open,
It's raging and crying,
What am I looking for?
What? What?

Trembling,
Anger's dying,
The sky is calming down.
A great sparkling treasure appears . . .
The sun.

Shona-Leanne Fenton (11)
Weyfield Primary School

A PIRATE'S TREASURE

Half buried in the sand
What is it?

A golden sparkle
A silver bowl
A dirty flag
A cracked skeleton
A smashed up skull

What is it?
The remains of a pirate and his treasure!

Russell Charman (10)
Weyfield Primary School

A LOST TREASURE

A moving treasure
A lost life

A silhouetted shadow
A silver sparkle

A wasted chance
A drastic measure

A missing link
A broken chain

A human's life
A lost treasure.

Riki Andrews (10)
Weyfield Primary School

HIDDEN TREASURE

Cave keeper,
Cave shaker,
Sand slider,
Money maker,
Gold giver,
Turtle taunter,
Floor mopper,
Coral clinger,
Treasure chanter,
Treasure trampler,
Water waker,
Fish finder,
Fish feeder.

Jamie Meyer-Scott (10)
Weyfield Primary School

WHERE IS IT?

Crying!
Looking for it,
I cannot find it now,
I am crying on my bed now,
Hunting.

Hoping!
Searching madly,
Think my life will end soon,
Finally there is my treasure,
Joyful.

Gleaming!
I am laughing,
Showing people it now,
My treasure is beautiful now,
Gold watch.

Darren Bierton (10)
Weyfield Primary School

THE QUEST

A pleasant light,
A wonderful shine.

A glamorous object,
A beautiful flyer.

An amazing cup,
A gold sparkle.

The Holy Grail.

#

Joshua Bailey (11)
Weyfield Primary School

HIDDEN TREASURES

This isn't sandy breadcrumbs -
Topped with a fizzy sea,
With a treasure trove,
And an ancient map,
Which is a title,
That never appears to me,
My little treasure,
Is naught but a hidden one,
But it's not one of those boxes crammed with gold,
It is a girl,
My precious jewel,
And my warmth of my blood hath ran cold,
For she is missing,
Oh, missing from my life,
She doesn't have a trail,
Or maybe a red cross in ink,
She is my only and dear treasure to me.
My life is torn in half,
By a treasure - how could you lose it?
It is gone from my heart,
It is gone forever to be.

Caroline Pady (10)
Weyfield Primary School

DIAMONDS AND RUBIES

A shiny gold charm.
Diamonds and rubies
In a dark chest
That lay on the sandy beach.
Hidden where the birds sleep.
Hidden well and can't be seen.

Night falls.
The wind blows
And carries the sand away.
And what's left?
A corner of a chest,
A brown pointy figure poking out of the sand.
Let's hope nobody finds it.

Rebecca Strudwick (10)
Weyfield Primary School

TREASURES OF THE WORLD

I am a photo under your bed.
I am a memory in your head.

I am the treasures in a tomb.
I am a locket lost in gloom.

I am the dream in your sleep.
I am the words that you keep.

I am the treasures lost in water.
I am more private than a porter.

I am the words you have written.
I am your long lost kitten.

I am your dark and deep desire.
I am that secret lost in fire.

I am your most loved pleasure.
I am your hidden treasure.

Bradley Mallett (11)
Weyfield Primary School

GREEK TREASURE

Under the ground is treasure,
Where the archaeologists measure.
There might be Greek pots or plates
Or even your dead mates!

Sometimes there is gold,
Or even something really old.
There might me rotten food
Or something or someone very rude.

Then I saw a faint glow,
I wondered what it wanted to show.
Then an evil curse came over me,
Suddenly I couldn't see!

Then I could see the glow again,
I thought it was some dead men.
But it was the Greek treasure - yes
Of course I made a big mess!

Liam Pratt (9)
Weyfield Primary School

THE EXTRA SHINY SAND

The sea crashes against the rocks.
The shiny stones shiver.
They sound like chattering teeth
Hitting the ground.
Footprints in the sand.
So deep,
There lies a diamond necklace . . .
I pick it up.
The sea goes silent once more.

Michelle Taylor (11)
Weyfield Primary School

Hidden Treasure

One hot morning we arrived in Greece,
my mum said on our holiday we were allowed to bring our niece.
In the morning we went to the beach to play with the sand,
when suddenly we dug so deep in the land.
We found something that glittered in the sun,
we tried to pick it up but it weighed a ton.
We finally got it and opened it,
my sister said it looked like a deep, deep black pit.
Inside there was lots of gold,
we thought no one has seen the treasure, it felt so cold.
We picked it up and put it in the car,
it was so heavy, we travelled so far.
When we got home everyone wanted to choose,
so the next day we were surprised to see that we were on the news.
And that was the end of the poem of hidden treasure.

Samantha Warren (10)
Weyfield Primary School

Where Is The Treasure?

Along came a tiny, tiny hand,
Searching for treasure under the sand.
Searching and searching is what it did,
But the treasure was far too well hid.
As the day grew older and older,
The pirate got colder and colder.
The pirate got bored,
And loudly he roared,
The treasure sank much more,
The pirate cried and flooded the shore!

Sadie Lewis (11)
Weyfield Primary School

A DULL BOX

A dull box
A small compartment

A pirate's dream
A deserted lot

A lost case
An abandoned chest

A mislaid trunk
A hidden crate

A private casket
A concealed package

But what's inside is much, much better

A shiny metal
A bright coloured necklace

Gold.

Sam Watts (11)
Weyfield Primary School

GREEK TREASURE POEM

I dug a hole and found a water vole
I dug some more and found an apple core
I dug the last and found some of the past
I dug a lot and found a Greek pot
I found a mask from the past
I found some gold wrapped in mould.

Shannon McWhinnie (10)
Weyfield Primary School

SHIPWRECKED TREASURE

A map
Of all the things.
Look, it says, 'treasure here'.
So I set off to the island.
I'm here.
Can't wait.
A long hike there.
It is underwater.
The treasure is on the shipwreck.
Through there.
I'm here.
There's the treasure.
Squeak! I open the box
Mortal powers that are so good.
Let's go!

Jake James (10)
Weyfield Primary School

THE TREASURE CHEST

T he island is huge.
R usty gold treasure chest.
E vil pirates made a trap.
A dark, gloomy cave full of skeletons.
S ecret maps are kept in bottles on the ocean.
U p on the volcano there is lava spitting out.
R ubies, gold chains, crystals and crowns.
E vil nasty sharks are eating pirates.
S cary bats are flying around in the cave.

Arron Nye (10)
Weyfield Primary School

HIDDEN TREASURE

As I looked across the golden sand
My crew and I looked around, shovels in hand.
X marks the spot, where could it be?
Why not check under the tall palm tree?
It was not there so we went ahead,
We found two sticks crossed like an X,
The deeper we dig, the harder it gets,
But I know we will find our treasure chest.
We were rewarded with silver and gold,
But one more problem, we left a big hole,
We filled it in and went on our way,
To sail the seas and to another day.

Terri-Lianne Brazil-Halls (10)
Weyfield Primary School

GOLDEN TREASURE

Look, look!
What have we found?
Try and open it quick!
It looks like a memory box
Who's that?

Creak, creak!
It is all dark.
Look at the bright gold
What shall we do with all of it?
Gold, silver!

Sian Young (11)
Weyfield Primary School

THE DRAGON'S HIDDEN TREASURE

In a big dark cave,
A dragon's hidden treasure saved,
For its comfort and where he laid,
And went to sleep in the shade.

His cave covered with gold,
That he will hold,
He had lots of treasure,
And so much pleasure.

He came out onto the sand,
And when he found . . .
A treasure box for his collection,
And had more protection.

The dragon rested,
It was the bested,
He was as long as a mile,
And he had a little smile.

Charlotte Bundy (9)
Weyfield Primary School

HIDDEN TREASURE

At last we have found the hidden treasure,
It gave us all a great pleasure!
It's white and gleams like gold,
It seems to be very old!
The treasure's in a dark, dark place,
Underground is where it lays!
Have you guessed what my treasure is?
My treasure's my bone, I'm a dog called Fiz.

Rebecca Gray (10)
Weyfield Primary School

HIDDEN TREASURE

Over the dusty hills,
Across the muddy grass,
Sailing across the water,
Slowly walking in the sand,
Mind the stones underneath your feet.
Oh look there's a chest in that boat.
Quick let's go across the windy, sandy beach,
Through the soft sand and we're there.
We slowly open the chest, we take a sneaky, peaky peak.
Oh look, there's a rugby that's twinkling in the sun,
A diamond shining in the moon.
Oh, look, it's an old treasure box from centuries ago.

Kirsty Salmon (9)
Weyfield Primary School

HIDDEN TREASURE

Cave keeper,
Haunted island,
Buried gold,
Cruel death,
Endless desert,
Dead pirates,
Clue taker,
Losing every step,
Sleeping and rotting
Souls.

Samantha Davies (10)
Weyfield Primary School

HIDDEN TREASURE

I was at a sunny hot island,
I looked around the massive island,
I went to the soft sand,
I put my feet in the breezy water,
I got my red shiny bucket and pink smooth spade,
I got my spade and dug,
All the sand went in different directions,
I felt something hard and bumpy,
I dug more to see what it was,
And I saw a rusty old box,
I picked up the big chest to see what it was,
It was heavier than a big bag of potatoes,
I opened the muddy worn-our rusty box,
It smelt like ancient rotten apples,
I was surprised to see two shiny tickets to Spain,
There was my hidden treasure.

Jade Spinks (9)
Weyfield Primary School

HIDDEN TREASURE

Glittering jewels, silver and gold.
Hidden in a place never to be told.
Buried deep down,
In a chest coloured brown.
Buried by pirates a long time ago.
They are the ones who really know.
But find their map and the place marked X
And you will discover the chest coloured brown.

Matt Kelly (10)
Weyfield Primary School

A BOX OF TREASURE

A massive box,
A lovely pattern,
A gold band,
A silver necklace,
A bronze ring,
A pile of money,
A pirate's head,
A box of jewellery,
A treasured story,
A fake bracelet,
A plastic coin,
A gold earing.

Tom Howard (11)
Weyfield Primary School

HIDDEN TREASURE

Treasure
treasure
gold
and
silver
hidden
under
the
sea
pirates
will
find
not
me.

Emma Ness (11)
Weyfield Primary School

HIDDEN TREASURE

Down in the deep dark forest,
Lay the treasure unknown,
Full of dark, dirty animals,
It was safely hidden away.

For good old captain Humbug,
Was closely on his path,
But in order for him to find it,
There was someone he must find.

Soon the dark day came,
The men departed from their homes,
Down the path of the winding forest,
They made it to the cross.

They dug, dug and dug,
Until something hit the rusty shovel,
Then, out came a small black box,
Which read,
The book of dead!

Jake Sullivan (11)
Weyfield Primary School

HIDDEN TREASURE

Hidden
Treasure in cave,
Twinkling sapphires,
Need a key to open treasure,
Diamonds.

Chantelle Dixon (11)
Weyfield Primary School

HIDDEN TREASURE

Today I feel very alive
Let's go for a plunge or a dive
Now I'm in the ocean, aqua blue
Although it's hard to swim through
I'm going deeper, deeper yet
I won't find anything, I won't even gamble or bet
Wait a minute, what have I found
On the seabed, we would call soily ground?
I should have guessed
It's a *treasure chest!*

I'll give my sister a coin or two or maybe three
She will still beg and plea
It's not the best
But I'll keep the remains and all the rest . . .
I know, I'll hide it and keep a coin or two
You won't tell anyone will you?

Sarah Bell (10)
Weyfield Primary School

SHIPWRECK'S TREASURE

S unken ships, broken bits, underwater sat a ship.
H itting against the jaggedy rocks, bits of wood hitting the docks.
I wanted to go and search the sea for at least one ruby.
P utting on the diving kit was tough, but when I'd done it
   I'd had enough.
W ater, water everywhere, then I felt a sudden scare.
R ubies lay on the ground, I stared and stared at what I'd found.
E verybody wanted to see what I found triumphantly.
C rashing still against the rocks is the wood upon the docks.
K ings wanted a peep at what I'd found in the deep.

Niall Campbell (9)
Weyfield Primary School

HIDDEN TREASURE

I search for something I cannot see,
I can feel it,
It's special to me,
I cannot touch it.
It makes me feel safe as can be,
It makes me happy.

It makes me feel warm inside
Like a hot water bottle,
It's difficult to hide,
Lots of hugs and cuddles,
It's having a family by my side,
I feel safe.

It's a kind of pleasure,
Lots of fun.
Seen without measure,
My family,
My hidden treasure,
Love!

Ruth Browton (10)
Weyfield Primary School

HIDDEN TREASURE

Treasure island is an island full of hidden treasure,
where people bathe upon gold sand and do things at their leisure.

And see all of the wonderful sights that fill you with awe and pleasure,
the giant sphinx, old Greek baths and pots, these are treasures
                                        you cannot measure.

Jasmine Blackburn (9)
Weyfield Primary School

HIDDEN TREASURE

As I walk along the sandy beach,
I feel something sharp below my feet,
It's pinky and shiny,
But not big nor tiny,
And it's sitting there not moving at all!

I slowly crouched down to see,
Something facing a completely different way to me,
And it's half buried under the sand,
It feels as cold as ice, and cost no price,
But to be honest the smell wasn't very amusing!

I've called it Sandie the shell,
And it does look like a bell,
Going side to side,
Ever since that day I've kept it with me,
But that revolting smell will always remind me
Of the sea!

Chelsey O'Mahoney (9)
Weyfield Primary School

HIDDEN TREASURE

My cousin has a diary
It also has a lock
She writes in it in pencil
Then puts it in a sock.

No one's allowed to look in it
She always seems to groan
And if anyone goes near her room
She always starts to moan.

She has a special hiding place
She found it at her leisure
The way she acts when I go round
You'd think her book was hidden treasure.

Paul Fenton (9)
Weyfield Primary School

HIDDEN TREASURE

The dogs in the dogs' home
Looked scruffy and sad
But when we took our dog home, he changed over night
He growled and barked and showed his teeth
To everyone except my dad
I always longed for a dog
I longed for him to love me
But the only time he liked me was when I gave him his food
I sat in the garden looking at him
He looked back and showed his teeth
Then a crash and a hand over my mouth
As quick as lightning
The dog was there
Biting the man's ankle
The man dropped me and ran away
The dog chased him off and came back to me
He liked me and I hugged him
He was now my dog
I called him Treasure because he is my treasure
He's my scruffy, wonderful dog!

Katherine Hope (9)
Weyfield Primary School

THE MAGIC TREASURE BOX

What do I want to put in my magic treasure box?

I will put the sound of water trickling down the stream,
the sound of a palm tree waving in the wind.
I will put the sound of a little baby's giggle,
the sound of a lion's great purr, *prrrrrr.*

I will put the sweet sound of the different sorts of birds,
singing in the morning,
the sound of an adult's boring conversation, time after time!

I will put the sweet scent of freshly cut red roses,
the beauty of a spring cut daffodil.
I will put the smell of fresh cut bright green grass,
the yummy taste of the bright orange carrots,
grown in your own garden.

Oh no! Here come the bad smells!

I will put the disgusting smell of my dad's armpit,
the smell of dry rabbit droppings.
The aroma of rotten apples just dangling on the last little twig.

Thank goodness! The good things are back!

I will put the sound of the bees flying around,
buzzzzzzz,
the sound of joy and laughter and all the happy things you can think of.

Well, that's all I can fit in my magic treasure box,
so I had better put the bright gold key back.

Jamie Varney (9)
Weyfield Primary School

HIDDEN TREASURE

I walked along a sandy beach,
I did it just for pleasure,
I came across a great big chest,
full of hidden treasure.

I touched the chest,
it was damp and cold,
I opened it up,
to find silver and gold.

I looked through the treasure,
and found a necklace and ring,
it must have belonged
to a queen or a king.

I was so excited,
I wanted to shout,
when I looked down the beach,
there was no one about.

I thought what to do,
for an hour and a day,
the only thing to do,
was to take it away.

No one was looking,
so I packed my bag,
it was so full and heavy,
that it started to sag.

My dad said, 'Great!
We'll hide it in our ditch.'
My mum said, 'Brilliant!
At last we'll be *rich!*'

James Stevens (10)
Weyfield Primary School

HIDDEN TREASURE

In my green-grassed garden,
I see my coal-black poodle running around,
He slowly walks up to my green apple tree.

He roughly barks three times,
Like he was doing a Morse code,
Then out came a tatty map,
Marked with an X.

He runs around, he goes up to the end of the garden,
He looks in the pond, he sees something floating,
He dives in!
He comes out soaking wet, biting a bone!

Taren Hewer (10)
Weyfield Primary School

HIDDEN TREASURE

Upstairs in my brightly coloured room,
In an old shoe box tied with a long purple ribbon,
Pictures and letters of Natalie.
A blonde-haired, blue-eyed girl,
My friend.
She left at the end of year four
To join another school.
All she left were happy memories,
Photographs of shared times,
Her photographs, letters, postcards and Christmas cards
Are my hidden treasure.

Jeysie Mallett (9)
Weyfield Primary School

HIDDEN TREASURE

As she opened the crackling wrapping paper,
She squealed with excitement,
She had been given a sparkling, gold locket,
She opened it up and saw a picture.

One hot day she ran straight into her house,
Her eyes were flooding with tears
She grabbed a tissue and snuffled,
She told me that she'd lost her precious locket.

So the next day I set off sailing,
When I saw something gold floating to shore,
Suddenly I got nearer and snatched it rapidly,
It was the gold, sparkling necklace.

I clenched it in my hand,
And rowed happily home with the locket,
When I got there I was so proud
To see this charming, fine lady hold it in her hand.

'Thank you!' she cried, smiling at me.
She hugged me tight
And made me biscuits and tea,
Then it was time to go home.

So the hidden treasure was the locket,
But at least I was best buddies with that lady!

Sarah Liddicott (10)
Weyfield Primary School

HIDDEN TREASURE

Old pirate Jack, he had one eye and stood on his peg leg.
He used to yell and shout a lot to everyone upon his boat.

They'd all get drunk on pirate rum that's given out by measures,
And sing all night about the maps of enormous hidden treasures.

They'd row their boat to some far shore to try and find the treasure,
Some would dig and some would climb but all sung with great pleasure.

But one-eyed Jack and all his men
Did never find the hidden treasure!

Bradley Carey (10)
Weyfield Primary School

IF I MOVED HOUSE

I would take my Christmas joys
And my imaginary friend
I would take the sound of blue tits chirping

I wouldn't take the old man over the road
Or the trains screeching into the station

I'd take the red roses across the road and the hurrying children
I'd take the weeping willow from behind the pond and the pond
                                    with its superb colours

I would not take the growling from next door
Or the memories of me watching Bob

I would take the big woods I run in!

Liam Jackman (9)
Worplesdon Primary School

IF I MOVED HOUSE

If I moved house I'd take:
My cosy space-age room,
My treehouse in my huge garden,
And the sound of the warm summer breeze
In the morning of every day

I wouldn't take:
The noise from the main road,
The weird sounds in Fairlands wood,
And I wouldn't take Mr Parsons (only kidding)

But I would take:
My very precious family.

Thomas Bates (9)
Worplesdon Primary School

IF I HAD

If I had wings
I would sit on fluffy clouds
And let the wind blow my thoughts away

If I had wings
I would taste the fruity rainbow
As I glide through the sky

If I had wings
I would fly to the moon

If I had wings
I would dream of walking with a shark
And swimming with a cat.

Elliot Mitchell (9)
Worplesdon Primary School

IF I MOVED HOUSE

If I moved house I'd take:
The tree me and my sister used to climb on
The time I actually had friends
The bells on the Christmas tree.

I wouldn't take:
The nettles in my neighbour's garden
The sound of my alarm clock
My friends' hatred game.

I'd take:
The good teaching from my teacher
The times I got what I wanted
The bathroom joys of privacy
My next door neighbour.

I wouldn't take:
The memories of my school horror
My friend's burnt food.

But I would take:
My cub leader.

Ben Beagley (9)
Worplesdon Primary School

IF I HAD FINS

I would touch the bottom of the wavy Pacific ocean,
I would taste the hard rocks as I swim past,
I would listen to the shoals of fish whooshing past.
I would smell the shark's bad breath as it tried to eat me.
I would look at the inside of a rock.
I would dream of a glittery crab floating past me.

Caroline Lowe (9)
Worplesdon Primary School

IF I MOVED HOUSE

If I moved house I'd take:
The family of foxes that lived in our garden
The walk down to the park on a winter's morning
And the sound of the wind on a November afternoon

But I wouldn't take:
The sound of people shouting when I'm trying to get to sleep
The baby next door
Or the creaky landing

I'd take:
The brightly painted shed
The green fence my cats climb on
And the times I opened my presents in my mum's bed
                                    and at my cousin's house.

Bryony Davison (10)
Worplesdon Primary School

IF I HAD WINGS

If I had wings
I would watch the people walking about.

If I had wings
I would fly over every country.

If I had wings
I would dream of
Walking the seas and
I would dream the
Rain was orange juice.

Jake Carey (9)
Worplesdon Primary School

COMMENTATING FOR A CLASS LESSON

And we're off and the teacher gets a pen.
She turns to the board. Is she going to write?
Yes! She has! What skill! That pen's moving madly!
But wait, what's this? She's stopped!
She points to the back of the classroom!
Oh! She shouts at a boy!
He storms off out of the classroom.
What a pity!
After such a great performance, too!
Oh, but she's started again.
Slightly slower.
Still going at a good pace, though.
But wait, something's happening. Could it be a . . .
Yes! A spelling mistake!
She rubs it out - wow! What a rub!
So fast!
It'll be over in no time if she keeps it up!
She sees the last line,
Steps up, writes,
Oh no! The bell's rang!
Only needed a few more words, too!
What a shame!
Well, back to the studio . . .

Alex Kingsbury (10)
Worplesdon Primary School

IF I HAD

If I had wings
I would go to the bright lights of Hollywood
and touch the moonlit sky.

If I had wings
I would glide over oceans without
a care.

If I had wings
I would blast into space
so see the stars.

If I had wings
I would walk in the sea
and swim through the forest.

Gregory Beaven (9)
Worplesdon Primary School

IF I MOVED HOUSE

If I moved house I'd take:
Every Christmas I had ever had.
The time when we had a family of hedgehogs in our garden.
The sound of the blue tits rustling in my neighbour's birdhouse.

If I moved house I wouldn't take:
The two dogs down my road who bark all night.
The time when my TV didn't want to work.
The time when my neighbours had a huge party
And played their music really loud and it came through the walls.

If I moved house I would take:
The warm summer evenings I spent playing with my friends.
The blossom tree in my back garden.
The sound of water flowing down a stream.

If I moved house I wouldn't take:
The cat next door who hates children.
My smoke alarm that goes off when I light a candle.
My garden, it's too messy.

But I would take my house filled with memories.

Katie Brooks (10)
Worplesdon Primary School

IF I HAD

If I had wings
I would fly up to the planets of the world
and flow through the midnight blue starry sky.

If I had wings
I would touch the tallest tree
and gaze down from up above.

If I had wings
I would get up close to animals
and hear them dreaming.

If I had wings
I would dream of
walking with dolphins
and swimming with grizzly bears.

Lucy Adams (10)
Worplesdon Primary School

IF I HAD WINGS

If I had wings
I would touch the sun's rays
If I had wings
I would taste the moon's cheese
If I had wings
I would listen to space
If I had wings
I would smell the raindrops in the clouds
If I had wings
I would gaze at the moon
If I had wings
I would dream of being a dolphin.

Michael Cook (9)
Worplesdon Primary School

IF I HAD

If I had Velcro feet
I would climb up the side of a building
and feel the wind's breath upon my face.

If I had Velcro feet
I would walk around the sun
and feel the sweat inside my shoes.

If I had Velcro feet
I would walk up the trees
and peer into the birds' nests.

If I had Velcro feet
I would dream of swimming up walls
and walking through seas.

Hayley Waugh (10)
Worplesdon Primary School

SNOW

I fall from the sky,
I am cold, soft and white.
I fall in the winter,
And make the world white.

You can throw me at people,
And make them all cold.
I am icy to touch,
And soft to hold.

Gregory Walsh (9)
Worplesdon Primary School

COMMENTATOR

Look at this
Fred Tuckey is doing something amazing
He's reaching for a dinner tray
The dinner lady's reaching for a spoon
The dinner lady has given him a bunch of chips
He's going like a train
He gets some pizza
Wow!
Now here comes the jelly
He runs out
Oh no
He's dropped the dinner tray
Looks like he will have to settle
With an apple and a biscuit.

Scott Greenfield (9)
Worplesdon Primary School

IF I HAD FINS

If I had fins I would
glide through the rainbow sea.

If I had fins I would
listen to the dolphins' secrets as they jumped into the air.

If I had fins I would
dream of walking in the sea and swim in the air.

Rosie Bowler (9)
Worplesdon Primary School

If I Had

If I had fins . . .
I would reach out to touch the multicoloured scales of the rainbow fish

If I had fins . . .
I would proudly taste the mouth-watering salt of the Pacific ocean

If I had fins . . .
I would love to hear the gentle breathing of the tropical fish

If I had fins . . .
I would sniff the bubbles from a coral reef and nervously pop them
one by one

If I had fins . . .
I would gaze excitedly down the side of coral, watching the bumps
rising up and down, whilst a shark sneaks past.

If I had fins . . .
I would dream of having wings and touching the top of the tallest tree
to watch the monkeys jump from tree to tree.

Rachel East (9)
Worplesdon Primary School

If I Had Wings

If I had wings I would reach out and touch the moon.
If I had wings I could leap up to taste an asteroid.
If I had wings I would stand and listen to the sun sizzle.
If I had wings I would smell the clouds as they go by.
If I had wings I would look down at the little pools of sea
                                        splashing every second.
If I had wings I would dream of swimming in the sea every day.

Robert Barham (10)
Worplesdon Primary School

If I Had Wings

If I had wings I would touch the gentle breeze of the wind
breathing on me.
If I had wings I would taste the freshest leaves on the highest tree.
If I had wings I would listen to the mountain snow as it shuffles
down the valleys.
If I had wings I would smell the cold moon as it shines at night.
If I had wings I would look at the beautiful stars sparkling in the sky.
If I had wings I would dream of swimming to the bottom of the
deepest ocean.

Nina Christie (9)
Worplesdon Primary School

If I Had Wings

If I had wings I would reach out and touch the sparkling snowflakes
as they gently hit the ground.
If I had wings I would love to taste the brightest colours of the rainbow.
If I had wings I would listen intently to a twister as it takes
everything with it.
If I had wings I would twitch my nose and smell the caves full of mist.
If I had wings I would fly over and look at the burning sun.
If I had wings I would dream of touching the bottom of the
deepest ocean.

Ellis Prior (9)
Worplesdon Primary School

IF I HAD WINGS

If I had wings
I would reach out to touch every plane that went by.

If I had wings
I would stretch to take the rain and drink it all, enjoying its fresh taste.

If I had wings
I would love to listen to the moon and stars as they came out at night.

If I had wings
I would sniff to smell the sun as it burnt my face.

If I had wings
I would gaze and look at foggy days.

If I had wings
I would dream and wonder at the day when I had no wings
                              and could swim with the dolphins.

Joshua Cook (9)
Worplesdon Primary School

IF I HAD WINGS

If I had wings I would fly to the moon and taste the cheese.
I would listen to the wind whispering in my ear.
I would smell the sweet scent of the trees' blossom.
If I had wings I would look at the sun burning to the water.
If I had wings I would dream of diving in the deepest sea ever.

Jamie Butler (9)
Worplesdon Primary School

IF I HAD WINGS

If I had wings
I would touch a tint of the misty cloud
which floats in the mid air.

If I had wings
I would taste the yellow burning sun
which stays still in the air.

If I had wings
I would listen to the lovely sweet birds
singing around me.

If I had wings
I would smell the invisible air
which never stops floating around us.

If I had wings
I would look down at the
little pale heads moving around.

If I had wings
I would dream again
of the lovely sky.

Selina Russel (10)
Worplesdon Primary School

IF I HAD GILLS

If I had gills
I would touch the belly of a whale without getting hurt.

If I had gills
I would excitedly taste the sandy bottom of the ocean
as crabs scuttle across it.

If I had gills
I would listen intently to the dolphins playing with each other.

If I had gills
I would love to smell the waves as they rush past.

If I had gills
I would carefully look at the inside of beautiful coral.

If I had gills
I would try to dream of a monkey fish.

Kate Bennett (9)
Worplesdon Primary School

IF I HAD WINGS

If I had wings
I would reach out to touch
the top branches of the tallest tree in the world.

If I had wings
I would love to taste
the soft furriness of the moving clouds.

If I had wings
I would listen enthusiastically to the sun
humming away gleefully as it beams down on the earth.

If I had wings
I would eagerly smell the sweetness
of the air as it dances around.

If I had wings
I would intently look at the people
scurrying down below to their houses.

If I had wings
I would silently dream of watching the interesting shapes
a centipede makes on the ground.

Georgina Pollard (9)
Worplesdon Primary School

IF I HAD WINGS

If I had wings
I would reach out and touch the sneaky fog
wandering through valleys.

If I had wings
I would lick my lips and taste the wind
hurrying through busy towns.

If I had wings
I would switch on my ears and listen
to the never-ending silence of the creepy woods at midnight.

If I had wings
I would take a deep breath and smell the rich scent of clouds
taking their time walking through the heavy mist.

If I had wings
I would strain my eyes and look at nature scurrying around
setting up for hibernation.

If I had wings
I would stare and dream of once again having no wings
and roaming the beautiful earth.

Pollyanna Jones (9)
Worplesdon Primary School

IF I HAD WINGS

If I had wings
I would fly to the moon and make castles
out of moon dust

If I had wings
I would fly round the world and gather up
the bad things

If I had wings
I would fly out of all my troubles

If I had wings
I would dream of
swimming the mountains
and walking the oceans.

Jessica Ruston (9)
Worplesdon Primary School

THE COMMENTATOR

And he's off.
Struggling to get the chair away from him.
Oh what movement!
Look at this!
Look at this!
He's trying to make his way to the computer.
He's dodging the chairs, jumping the tables.
Oh he's made it to the computers.
He's on his way back.
But wait, he's slipping.
Oh! But he's back up again.
What courage.
It takes a lot for this man to go down.
Oh my God!
What is this?
A chair is falling over!
He's putting his brakes on, just in the nick of time!
Oh Mr Armand sees him
But wait!
Thomas Sands has opened the door and knocked Mr A spark out.

Tony Page
Worplesdon Primary School